Florence Nightingale and the Viceroys

*A Campaign for the
Health of the Indian People*

Gitanjali, Stanza 35

Where the mind is without fear
And the head is held high;
Where knowledge is free;
Where the world has not been broken up
    into fragments by narrow domestic wars;
Where words come out from the depths of truth;
Where tireless striving stretches its arms
towards perfection;
where the stream of reason has not lost its way
into the dreary desert sand of dead habits;
where the mind is led forward by thee into
ever-widening thought and action
into that heaven of freedom, my Father, let my
    country awake.

Rabindranath Tagore

Sir Rabindranath Tagore
(1861–1941)

'Tagore was a poet, educator and, above all a humanist
. . . he did not think that India belonged to one race
or religion. His marked sincerity, beauty of political
expression and love of humanity had widespread influence all over the world.'

D P Singhal,
A History of the Indian People (Methuen, 1983)

Florence Nightingale and the Viceroys

A Campaign for the
Health of the Indian People

Patricia Mowbray

HAUS
BOOKS
London

Originally published in Great Britain
in 2008 by Haus Publishing Limited
26 Cadogan Court, Draycott Avenue, London SW3 3BX

The moral right of the author has been asserted
A CIP catalogue record for this book is avail: le
from the British Library

ISBN 9781905791231

Designed and typeset in Baskerville MT
by Ellipsis Books Limited, Glasgow

Cover image courtesy of the Florence Nightingale Museum
Printed and bound by Graphicom, Vicenza, Italy

www.hauspublishing.co.uk

Contents

Introduction

Lytton Strachey published *Eminent Victorians* in 1918 with the intention of knocking an assortment of famous Victorians off their pedestals. In his essay on Florence Nightingale, brilliantly combining fact with myth, waspish criticism with reluctant praise, he wrote: "For many years it was de rigueur for the newly appointed Viceroy, before he left England, to pay a visit to Miss Nightingale."

The link between the Viceroys – ten were appointed between the years 1858 and the turn of the century – and a frail middle-aged woman, plagued by intermittent bouts of fever after service in the Crimea, was the extraordinary knowledge she had accumulated of conditions affecting the health of the Indian people, particularly the rural poor. Her battle cry for action to each newly appointed Viceroy was "*Sanitation! Irrigation!*"

Florence Nightingale attached great importance to this last mission. In a note enclosed with her will, she asked that the relevant papers should not be destroyed. Her accredited biographer, Sir Edward Cook, described it as "one of the heaviest and most useful pieces of work she ever did". It is therefore surprising that a trawl through six contemporary histories of India produced only one rather dismissive reference: a brief mention of her lengthy correspondence with the distinguished Indian administrator, Sir Bartle Frere. It was, however, reassuring to have my attention drawn to *Florence Nightingale and the Health of the Raj* by Jhanna Gourlay (2003). This work, based upon an impressive body of research, provides new insights into Florence Nightingale's wide-ranging contacts on the Indian continent with major participants in the struggle for self-rule and associations concerned with education, land tenancy and other social issues.

My aim – more narrowly – is to explore the results of Miss Nightingale's collaboration over forty years with a remarkable procession of British statesmen who, during a significant period of change, held the lives of millions of Indians in their hands.

Acknowledgements

I am indebted to my editor, Robert Pritchard, for his belief in this book and for his exhortation to "keep writing"; and to David Gentleman for his willingness to contribute artwork. I am also grateful to Derek Marsden for the introduction to Haus Publishing.

Special thanks are due to Professor Anthony and Mrs Elizabeth Mellows for their friendship and support, not only during the last three years, but also for their faith in the Florence Nightingale Museum project and generous provision of much-needed funds during the early years.

I owe a great debt of gratitude to the members of my support team: Oxford friends and advisers, Bruce and Anne Wilcock, for essential guidance on style and presentation; John Kirchner for his patient transformation of my draft into presentable text; Iain Mulligan for introducing me to the British Library, and help in wide-ranging research; Barbara Purvis for recalling her work with FAO/UN in

rural areas of India and for access to her book collection;
Yvonne Hibbert for her encouragement and an introduction to members of staff of the Bodleian Library;
Lucinda Ganderton for practical information essential to
a first-time author.

Grateful thanks are also due to: Miss M S Travis, Hon
Librarian, High Commission of India Library, for material on the poet Rabindranath Tagore; to Eamonn Duigan
of Mayo House, Co Meath, and to Brian McCabe, Kill
Local History Group, Johnstown, Co Kildare for their
help with research on the life of Lord Mayo.

I acknowledge with gratitude the assistance so willingly
given by the staff of the following libraries and institu-
tions: Bodleian Library, British Library, Cambridge
University Library, Florence Nightingale Museum Library,
National Portrait Gallery, Muniment Room and Library
Westminster Abbey, Richmond (Surrey) Reference Library,
Muniment Room and Library, and to the staff of my
local Kew Library for handling weighty biographies from
the excellent Inter-Library Loan Service.

And finally I wish to thank friends and relatives in this
country and abroad who have been in close touch every
step of the way over the past three years.

Chapter 1

Florence Nightingale – The Last Campaign

DEATH OF SIDNEY HERBERT, AUGUST 1861

The death of the man Florence Nightingale thereafter referred to as her "Master" drew a line under an extraordinary chapter in her life. She first met Sidney and Elizabeth Herbert in Rome during the winter of 1847–48 where they were spending an extended honeymoon. The three found they shared humanitarian interests and became close friends.

Seven years later Herbert, now Secretary-at-War in Lord Aberdeen's government, wrote officially asking Miss Nightingale to lead an expedition of nurses to the Crimea: "There is but one person in England that I know of who would be capable of organizing and superintending such a scheme . . .". His letter, dated 15 October 1854, crossed

a note from Florence to Elizabeth Herbert giving news of a plan that she should take a privately financed group of nurses to Scutari. But Herbert's request prevailed and six days later Florence Nightingale and her party of thirty-eight nurses left for the Crimea.

Following fruitful collaboration on army matters in the post-Crimean years, Sidney Herbert was forced in December 1860 to tell Florence that failing health meant there was an urgent need to cut down on his commitments. His wife, with support from Florence, persuaded him to resign his ministerial office and accept a peerage (Lord Stanley of Lea) with a seat in the House of Lords.

But Florence pressed her friend to continue work on their current campaign for the health of the British army in India; she did not believe in "fatal diseases". Her percep-tive biographer, Sir Edward Cook, wrote "she sometimes

Arthur Hugh Clough

Sidney Herbert a portrait by Richmond

attributed to infirmity of will what was in fact infirmity of body. And her grief when the end came was not free of guilt."

The crippling sense of loss and desolation was compounded that same year by the death of a much-loved younger relative by marriage, the gentle Arthur Hugh Clough, a faithful companion and assiduous performer of a variety of useful tasks essential to the smooth running of her life.

CAMPAIGN FOR THE HEALTH OF THE ARMY IN INDIA

Withdrawal to lodgings in Hampstead severed Florence Nightingale's long connection with No.30 Old Burlington Street in the heart of London where the "kitchen cabinet" had worked tirelessly to achieve a Royal Commission for the health of the army at home. *"Our Soldiers Enlist to Die in Barracks"* was Miss Nightingale's call for improved sanitary conditions and the benefits were impressive.

During the winter of 1861–2 Florence's health gave serious cause for alarm, but slowly she regained strength. Friends encouraged her to resume the work she had shared with Sidney Herbert and there were offers of support from Sir Hugh Rose, Commander-in-Chief of the Army in India, and Lord de Grey, recently reappointed Under-Secretary for War and a dedicated reformer. She found new working quarters in London and set to work with renewed zest.

It had recently been revealed that there was an average of 69 deaths per 1,000 soldiers serving in India, with more dying from disease than on the battlefield. After strenuous lobbying, the Royal Sanitary Commission on the Health of the Army in India was approved by Queen Victoria in 1859 with Herbert as Chairman – all too soon to be succeeded by Lord Stanley. Florence had a voice in the nomination of members, including a sanitary expert, Dr Sutherland, and the eminent statistician, Dr Farr, who formed her new team.

A circular of enquiry was drawn up and despatched to every military station in India requiring full statistical information about conditions in the barracks and surrounding areas. As Sir Edward Cook dryly observed: "Dr Farr's appetite for statistics was as impassioned as hers" (Miss Nightingale's). The completed reports came flooding back to London for assessment by the working party and, finally in May 1863 the Commission's 'Report and Recommendations' (2028 pages) was adopted, together with a further paper '*The Observations of Miss Nightingale*' (28 pages) and were widely circulated by means of a staged publicity campaign orchestrated by Florence. Unusually, for a report printed by Her Majesty's Stationery Office, the '*Observations*' were illustrated with plans for improved army barracks and lively woodcuts of a female street sweeper and water and refuse carriers by Hilary Bonham Carter, based on sketches sent from India. (Miss Nightingale met the extra cost.) The '*Observations*' also contained extracts from the station reports which make uncomfortable reading. She assessed the main causes of disease to be bad water, bad drainage, filthy bazaars, and

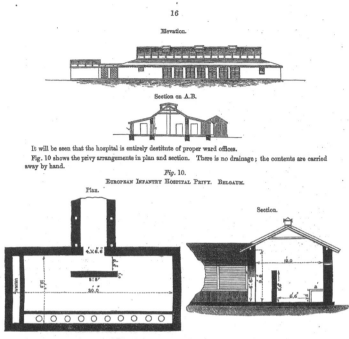

16

Elevation.

Section on A.B.

It will be seen that the hospital is entirely destitute of proper ward offices.
Fig. 10 shows the privy arrangements in plan and section. There is no drainage; the contents are carried away by hand.

Fig. 10.
EUROPEAN INFANTRY HOSPITAL PRIVY. BELGAUM.

Plan.

Section.

Fig. 11 shows a somewhat better construction of hospital, but there is the same defect in detail.

An architectural drawing for improved barrack hospital sanitation

want of ventilation in overcrowded barrack huts and sick bays. She did not mince her words and her ironic comments on the station reports provide a welcome touch of humour, for example: *"Drainage which we have found necessary for health in this colder climate is by no means necessary for health in the hot climate of India . . . most of the reporters find no drainage a sufficient guarantee of health."* And again: *"In times past there has been no proper sanitary service in India. No doubt there has been more or less of cleanliness; because wherever Englishmen go they attend to this one way or another."*

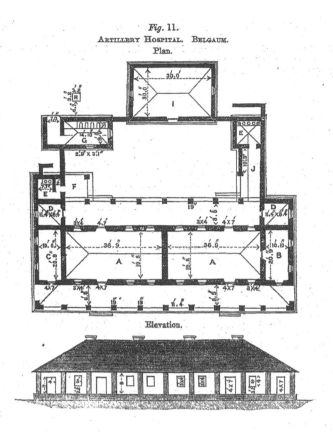

Elevation and plans for a new military hospital at Belgaum

"HOW PEOPLE MAY LIVE AND NOT DIE IN INDIA."

The case for the army in India had been made. Sir John McNeill, a doctor Florence Nightingale had worked with in the Crimea, wrote in August 1862: "The picture is terrible, but it is all true. There is no one statement from beginning to end that I feel disposed to question . . .". However, her suggestions for reform were

An idealised representation of a Barrack room interior in India

not always accepted by the government of the day.

The proposal for a Sanitary Department in the India Office was opposed, but a Sanitary Committee was eventually set up in the Army Office which Florence hailed as *"the dawn of a new day for India in sanitary things, not only as regards our Army, but as regards the native population."* Her mind was turning to the needs of the Indian people in towns, in civil hospitals, but above all in the impoverished rural areas. The way forward had already been signposted by Sir Charles Trevelyan, Governor of Madras, in a letter dated 11 August 1862: "In this case you are doing much more than providing for the health of the Troops; for, to be effectual, the improvements must extend to the civil population and thus another great element of civilisation will be introduced."

Later that year Trevelyan was appointed Financial Member of the Council of India. He promised to give

INDIAN DRAINAGE SYSTEM.

Hilary Bonham-Carter's drawing of one of the systems of Indian drainage

continuing support and asked for a copy of the Abstract of Evidence attached to the Sanitary Commission's report, highlighting points of particular importance; Florence promptly sent enough papers to keep him fully occupied on his sea voyage to India! Subsequently it was suggested that she might visit India as the guest of the Trevelyans, but she never saw the country.

Florence Nightingale's paper entitled *"How People may live and not die in India"* was read at a meeting of the National Association for the Promotion of Social Science held in Edinburgh in October 1863 and fully reported in *The Scotsman*. 250 copies of the paper were printed as a pamphlet for private circulation by Emily Faithfull, Printer and Publisher in Ordinary to Her Majesty (Appendix A). A further edition was published by Longmans in August 1864 and widely circulated in Britain and India.

From 1863 until the end of the century Florence worked with passion for the health of the Indian people, stressing the vital need for pure water and sanitation, reinforced by the appointment of more sanitary officers, and calling for the installation of irrigation works to control the unending cycle of drought, famine and disease. More supporters rallied to the cause, among them Sir John Lawrence, who had ruled so successfully in the Punjab and would become the third Viceroy.

The appointment of Viceroys from 1858 provided a further sphere of influence. Most – but perhaps not all – valued Miss Nightingale's unrivalled knowledge of conditions in India; she needed their power.

A portrait of Florence Nightingale by George Richmond

Chapter 2

The First Viceroys:
Lords Canning and Elgin (8th Earl)

TRANSFER OF BRITISH RULE IN INDIA TO THE CROWN

The shock waves of the Indian Mutiny in 1857 led to an extensive reorganisation of the way the British ruled India for the next sixty years. A proclamation by Queen Victoria in 1858 undertook on behalf of the imperial government to "respect the rights, dignity and honour of native princes as our own" in recognition of their loyal support during the Mutiny. The Prince of Wales made a royal progress through the country in 1875 and in 1877 the Queen took the title "Empress of India".

Lord Canning, then Governor-General, became Viceroy as personal representative of the Monarch, with direct responsibility to the Secretary of State and Council of India – an arrangement that would lead to complex relations and voluminous correspondence between Calcutta and London. There was, however, tacit agreement that the Viceroy should not become involved in party politics.

The term of office was up to five years except "in the case of misadventure"; for example, the assassination of Lord Mayo and Lord Lytton's recall because of his embroilment in the Afghan wars. In India the Viceroy had to rely on the grassroots experience of the British administrators. These were remarkable men who worked with the Indian rulers to achieve a balanced and benevolent rule of law and justice for all. It was usual for an administrator to be seconded to the Viceroy; for example Sir Bartle Frere, who served both Lords Canning and Lawrence with unswerving loyalty.

Unlike the Indian civil servants who were recruited by competitive examination, the Viceroys were chosen by the Cabinet of the day. Their background was, in the main, impeccably aristocratic: a peerage was bestowed with the posting. Knowledge of an Indian language was deemed unnecessary. They could not own property in India or take part in trade.

In spite of the prestige involved it was not always easy to find willing recruits. The risks to the health of wives and children had to be considered and there would be heavy financial demands on the Viceroy's private resources. He was required to meet the cost of fares and transport of personal baggage to India and to buy all plate, wine, carriages and horses from the outgoing Viceroy. And there was also the matter of the Vicereine's trousseau and jewellery, which had to go some way to matching the splendour of the Indian princes. Maintenance of huge staffs at the Viceregal Lodge in Calcutta and the summer residence at Simla would have absorbed a large part of the Viceroy's salary. The formal entertainments far outstripped the simpler regime at Buckingham Palace and Windsor Castle.

On a wider scale there were always looming crises to be dealt with: droughts, floods, famine, the unruly Afghans, the encroaching Russians . . . Small wonder there was no rush of candidates coming forward: but forward they came – "a stately procession . . . hiding behind its pageantry many controversies and much activity".

The First Viceroys

LORD CANNING [1858–62];
THE 8TH EARL OF ELGIN [1862–3]

The Lords Canning and Elgin are peripheral figures in the life of Florence Nightingale; their vice-regal appointments preceded Florence Nightingale's campaign for the health of the Indian people. But they would certainly have been aware of her Crimean reputation and her herculean efforts to improve barrack conditions for the British troops in India. Their links with her are seemingly slight – but not uninteresting – and their achievements cannot be ignored.

LORD CANNING (1818–1862)

"For the British at the time of the Mutiny and for decades after, Canning stood for faith always as the Saviours of the Raj, high on the list of those great officers of state whose services to their country entitle them to the esteem and gratitude of every loyal Englishman."

Lord Canning in 1860

Charles John Canning was born in west London, third son of the acclaimed George Canning, a disciple of Pitt, who served as Foreign Secretary in Lord Greville's Tory government during the Peninsular War in Spain (1808–13) and subsequently as a Prime Minister famed for his oratory. The Canning family was of Anglo-Irish descent; Charles Canning's mother had Scottish forebears. Charles was educated at a private school in Putney, then at Eton College, and entered Christ Church, Oxford, in December 1829, gaining a first class honours degree in classics and a second in mathematics. His contemporaries included Gladstone and the Lords Dalhousie and Elgin.

In 1835, at the age of twenty-three, Charles Canning married Charlotte Stuart, the eighteen-year-old daughter of Lord Stuart de Rothesay, and the following year entered politics as Tory member for Warwick. His two elder brothers died young and, on the death of his mother in March 1837, Charles succeeded to the peerage created in her favour after the death of her husband, taking his seat as Viscount Canning of Kilbracken, County Kilkenny. He was appointed Under-Secretary of State for Foreign Affairs in Sir Robert Peel's Conservative government until its collapse in 1846, and thereafter held a succession of political posts, earning a reputation for sound judgment based on painstaking research.

Lord Canning replaced Lord Dalhousie as Governor General of India on 29 February 1856. During a period of relative stability Dalhousie had introduced new administrative structures, established the first railways and the telegraph (which would prove a vital means of communication during the Indian Mutiny), and had some success in reducing the powers of the Indian princes in favour of the peasants.

An uprising in Moultan in 1848 and the death of two Europeans had given some cause for alarm and Lord Canning, in an address to the directors of the East India Company before he left for India, warned: "We must not forget that in the sky of India, serene as it is, a cloud may arise, at first no bigger than a man's hand, but which growing larger and larger, may at last threaten to burst and overwhelm us with ruin."

One year later the Mutiny erupted; Lord Canning's firm rule as Governor-General and Viceroy during and in the aftermath of the violence, and his collaboration with Sir John Lawrence on military tactics, will be explored in the following chapter.

Lord Canning, from all accounts, was not a sociable man, variously described as "austere, aloof" and "taciturn". The link with Miss Nightingale came through his wife. Following their early marriage, which proved childless, Lady Canning – as with many aristocratic women in the Victorian age – divided her days between the demands of life in high society and involvement in benevolent causes for the poor. For thirteen years she served as a Lady of the Bedchamber to Queen Victoria, a great favourite with both the Queen and Prince Albert. The appointment entailed waiting on the Queen three times a year for short periods – both at home and abroad – leaving ample opportunity for

Charlotte Canning at her drawing desk, Calcutta 1861

development of her artistic skills and good works.

As Chairwoman of the Council for the Institution for the Care of Sick Gentlewomen in Distressed Circumstances, Lady Canning was instrumental in the appointment of Florence Nightingale as superintendent of the Institution, with responsibility for finding and equipping a suitable house, finally established at No. 1 Harley Street. This was Florence Nightingale's first situation (unpaid), achieved in the face of stiff opposition from her mother and sister, but with financial support and quiet encouragement from her father. She was required to work with two committees, one of "Ladies" and the other of "Gentlemen". Miss Nightingale found the ladies troublesome and preferred working with the gentlemen. Lady Canning proved a strong ally and the work went well. Miss Nightingale developed her administrative and nursing skills, and mastered the art of managing committees, writing to her father in December 1853: *"When I entered service here, I determined that, happen what would, I never would intrigue among the Committees. Now I perceive I do all my business by intrigue."*

Lady Canning's collaboration with Florence Nightingale continued during the Crimean War when she joined forces with Sidney Herbert's wife in the selection of nurses for the campaign. Between the months of April and September 1855 she received regular and very witty reports from Florence Nightingale on the progress (or otherwise) of the nurses despatched to Scutari.

Lord Canning was appointed Governor-General of India on 29 February 1856. His wife, Charlotte, was well suited to her new role. Her father, Sir Charles Stuart (later Baron Stuart de Rothesay), was British Ambassador in Paris at the time of her birth; her mother a daughter of the Third Earl of Hardwicke. Charlotte was poised, pious, and very beautiful: the German portraitist of European royal families, Franz Winterhalter, painted her portrait. She was eager to explore aspects of Indian life and landscape, unlike her reclusive husband who – weighed down with paperwork – seldom found time to accompany his wife on expeditions.

But there were always lively young aides-de-camp only too willing to ride with her.

Throughout her years in India Lady Canning sent vivid accounts of her daily life and activities to family and friends; and also to Queen Victoria, who found much of interest in the letters. A gifted artist, she spent many hours sketching and produced a charming portfolio of drawings of the native trees and flowers. She also planned the development of the gardens at their residence at Barrackpore, outside Calcutta, a place she loved.

During the Mutiny Lord and Lady Canning maintained

Lady Canning and her retinue on an elephant at Futtehghur, 1859

An early Victorian painting of the entrance to Barrackpore

a stoic presence in Calcutta. There were the usual entertainments at Government House to keep up morale in a
city increasingly under threat from the rebels. With the aid
of a team of tailors and seamstresses Lady Canning produced
clothes for a stream of refugees and is said to have given
away much of her splendid trousseau to the wives of army
officers and officials. She also supervised arrangements for
care of the wounded. In a letter to her mother dated 14
November 1858 Lady Canning refers to a remarkable offer
from Florence Nightingale: ". . . she (Miss Nightingale) is
out of health at Malvern, but says she would come at twenty-
four hours' notice if I think there is anything to do in her
line of business. I think there is not anything here for there
are few wounded men in want of actual nursing, and there

are plenty of servants and assistants who can do the dressings. Only one man, who was very ill of dysentery, has died since we went to the hospital a fortnight ago. The up-country hospitals are too scattered for a running establishment, and one could hardly yet send women up." Miss Nightingale made the offer twice, once through Mr Sidney Herbert and then in a personal letter carried by her cousin, Major Nicholson, who was reporting for service in India. She was deeply involved in work for the army at home, but would have felt that active service in the field should take precedence. Had the offer been accepted sheer willpower might have sustained her, but she was still suffering from the effects of her severe illness in the Crimea; a nursing home in Malvern was her bolthole when the fever struck.

With the rebellion crushed, Lord Canning was elevated to an earldom and appointed first Viceroy of India. He travelled widely, holding durbars at Lucknow, Cawnpore, Agra, Lahore and other particularly sensitive areas. The Vicereine accompanied him on a number of these journeys, although she disliked camp life. She longed to return to England, but the Viceroy's term had been extended; finally a date for his retirement was set in January 1862. In October 1861 Lady Canning made an expedition to the borders of Sikkim in the Himalayas, hoping for a glimpse of Mount Everest. On the return journey she fell ill with jungle fever – a severe form of malaria. Lord Canning had been away for a presentation of the new Order of the Star of India; he hastened back to Calcutta to be with his wife. She died ten days later on 18 November 1861 and was

Canning holding a Durbar at Cawnpore

A view of the grounds at Barrackpore near Lady Canning's grave

A view of Barrackpore

buried in the garden at Barrackpore. Lord Canning was clearly distraught and in poor health. He handed over the viceroyalty to Lord Elgin on 12 March 1862 and returned to London a broken man. A disease of the liver was diagnosed; death followed swiftly on 17 June 1862 and he was buried with full honours in Westminster Abbey.

Queen Victoria added a mournful footnote. She had heard of Lady Canning's death while Prince Albert lay dying, and when Lord Canning's death followed seven months later she wrote: "How enviable to follow so soon the partner of your life! How I pray it may be God's will to let me follow mine soon!" But it was not to be.

JAMES BRUCE, EIGHTH EARL OF ELGIN AND TWELFTH EARL OF KINCARDINE (1811–1863) VICEROY 1862–63

"A man of courage and ability who served the Empire for over twenty years but deplored what he called the 'commercial ruffianism' which effectively determined British policy responses."

In photographs the eighth Lord Elgin, despite his ancient Scottish titles, does not present a romantic figure, but he has a unique place in the history of British imperialism as the man who set fire to the Emperor's summer palace in Peking.

James Bruce was the eldest of eight children from his father's second marriage to Elizabeth, daughter of James Oswald of Dunnikier House, Kirkcaldy, Fife. The first marriage to Mary Hamilton Nisbet had ended in a notorious divorce; their eldest son was heir to the titles and estates but, on his premature death in 1840, James Bruce became the heir. His father, Thomas Bruce, seventh Earl of Elgin, in the course of a Grand Tour, had purchased the Parthenon marbles and sold them to the British Government for a less than equitable price, thereby depleting his fortune and condemning his combined family of thirteen children, five from the first marriage and eight from the second, to an impoverished upbringing in Paris.

James Bruce was educated at Eton and Christ Church, Oxford, graduating in 1832 with a first in classics. For some years he helped to manage the family estates at

Broomhall in Fife. Financially it was unrewarding; a career in politics seemed preferable. After an unsuccessful bid for the Fife conservative seat, he was elected in August 1841 as a 'conservative with liberal tendencies' for Southampton. Later that year, having made his first speech in the House of Commons, James Bruce succeeded on the death of his father to the titles of Elgin and Kincardine. As a Scottish peer he could not remain in the Commons, and might only take his seat in the Lords after election by twelve representative Scottish peers.

Following his marriage in April 1841 to Elizabeth, daughter of Major C L Cumming Bruce, MP, Elgin accepted the post of Governor of Jamaica – the first step in a career of imperial administration that would lead him to Canada, Japan, China, and finally India.

On the voyage to Jamaica Lord and Lady Elgin were involved in a shipwreck. A nursemaid sent out from England died. It was not a propitious beginning. The birth of a daughter was followed by the young mother's prolonged illness and eventual death in 1843. Throughout this period of private grief Lord Elgin grappled with Jamaica's seemingly intractable problems. Slavery had been abolished throughout the British Empire in 1833, but a requirement that former slaves in Jamaica should continue to work for their masters as "apprentices" led to endless unrest, with the workers demanding their freedom and the planters refusing to compromise. Finally, in the spring of 1846, Lord Elgin retired from the governorship and returned to Scotland with his small daughter, Elma. A second marriage to Lady Mary Louisa Lambton, eldest daughter of the Earl of Durham, brought new happiness, stability for his motherless child, and, in due course, five more children.

CANADA

In February 1847 Lord Elgin sailed to Canada to take up the post of Governor-in-Chief of British North America. There had been unrest in the country in 1837 and 1838. Lord Durham was sent out to report on the

8th Earl Elgin

situation and recommended union of Upper and Lower
Canada. The hope was that this would lead to independence, but the hostility between the Anglo-Scots and
the rebellious French-Canadians did not abate.

Lord Elgin's initial task was to reconcile the two groups,
but his announcement in Parliament that the official
languages of the country would henceforward be English
and French (he spoke in both languages) brought a furious
reaction from the Anglo-Scots and there was further opposition to the Rebellious Losses Bill which allowed payment
of compensation to those whose property had been
damaged in the riots of 1837–8. The parliament building
in Montreal was demolished, the Governor-General's
carriage stoned, and Lord Elgin and his family retired to

Lord Elgin is stoned by an angry mob in Montreal

their official residence outside the capital. He remained resolute and his firm handling of the crises eventually brought calm to the troubled country.

Lord Elgin then set off on an extensive tour, making himself accessible to people of all shades of opinion, and although not by nature outgoing, succeeded in gaining their respect and trust. His final action was to negotiate a reciprocity agreement with the United States which underlined Canada's status within the British Empire.

On completing seven years' service Lord Elgin returned to England. Two sons had been born in Canada, and Queen Victoria, as an expression of her approval of the father's governorship, stood sponsor for the elder boy, Victor Alexander Bruce. He, in turn, would become the ninth earl and tenth Viceroy of India.

CANTON AND JAPAN

For the next eighteen months Lord Elgin enjoyed a peaceful family life. He attended debates in the House of Lords, but was not drawn to a life of politics. In 1857 he accepted the offer of an appointment as high commissioner and plenipotentiary in China and the Far East, with a remit to improve relations with China and Japan and open up trading opportunities in those countries. He sailed for the East in April 1857 with overall command of a large military and naval force to strike fear into the hearts of the Chinese, but was deeply troubled by the seemingly aggressive nature of his mission.

On arriving in Singapore Lord Elgin found urgent messages from the Governor-General of India, Lord Canning, asking him to despatch troops to help in suppressing the Mutiny. Elgin immediately ordered his ships to proceed to India, where the British troops relieved the beleaguered garrisons at Lucknow and Calcutta.

The move against Canton came later in the year when Elgin had reassembled his regiments. Initially he tried to mediate with Governor Ye for a British trading base, but eventually was forced to follow the preferred policy of aggression and gave the order for attack. After a bombardment lasting twenty-seven hours Canton fell to the British and Governor Ye was taken prisoner. In a letter to his wife Lord Elgin confessed: "I never felt so ashamed of myself in my life."

The action then moved to Shanghai where, after months of prevarication and broken promises, the Treaty of Tientsin was signed in June 1858. Relatively peaceful negotiations with the Japanese followed, and within a month Lord Elgin had secured a trade treaty with the Japanese. Whereas there had been a muted reaction to his diplomacy in Canada, he now came home to widespread praise for his successful exploits in the Far East and, above all, his support for Lord Canning during the Indian Mutiny. But this belated recognition brought little pleasure. Elgin deeply regretted that his objectives had been achieved, not by mediation, but by the use of armed force.

Lord Elgin was created Grand Commander of the Order of the Bath in 1858, served briefly as Postmaster General, and was elected Lord Rector of the University of Glasgow in 1859. But events in China took a worrying turn: his brother, Frederick Bruce, had been appointed minister for China and, while making his way by ship up the Peiho River, had come under attack from Chinese forces. The British suffered heavy losses and were forced to retreat.

Lord Elgin agreed to lead a mission directed at Peking; he was supported by an army of 30,000 men with an additional 10,000 troops from France. He faced major problems. China was not a state in the Western sense. The Emperor was a godlike figurehead, used by various factions to further their own machinations. Provincial governments were lax and corrupt, unlikely to respond to the rites of Western diplomacy. In addition, Lord Elgin was at odds with Harry Parkes, the British consul in Canton, and his coterie of "empire builders" and traders, all favouring a policy of aggression and unwilling to compromise. He disliked what he termed their "commercial ruffianism", but a meeting with Parkes in Hong Kong went some way towards bridging the gulf between them.

After landing in China Lord Elgin led his troops straight to Tientsin. He was unyielding in his demands and eventually the Chinese allowed British ministers to enter Peking. The Treaty was ratified and Tientsin became an open port. The British and French forces proceeded to Tung-Chow, a few miles from Peking. There news reached them that a party of thirty British and French envoys – including Harry Parkes and Henry Loch (Lord Elgin's private secretary) – had been taken hostage. They had been brutally treated and only five had survived; Elgin demanded their release but a stalemate ensued and he decided to burn down the Emperor's summer palace on the outskirts of Peking. Six days later his troops entered the city; the captives (including Parkes and Loch) were released and Frederick Bruce was proclaimed the Queen's representative in China.

So ended Lord Elgin's two missions to China, which had far-reaching consequences for British trade and diplomatic relations in the Far East. In Britain there was general acclaim for his achievements, although there were inevitably some who denounced the destruction of the Summer Palace. Yet Elgin had striven throughout the negotiations to show "mercy and justice to the people of China and infinite compassion for their needs", and on this occasion felt no remorse.

INDIA (1862–3)

Lord Elgin returned to Britain in April 1861 and the following November was offered the role of Viceroy of India in succession to Lord Canning. He accepted the appointment, but was aware of the many problems that must be faced in the wake of the Mutiny. At the age of fifty-one he might well have chosen to lead a peaceful and reasonably useful life in his own country. Over twenty years spent handling crises in widespread areas of the British Empire, with extreme variations of climate, had weakened his health and he sailed for India with a strong premonition that he would not return.

In a *Punch* cartoon Lord Elgin threatens to bombard Peking in 1860

The induction ceremony was held in Calcutta on 12 March 1862. Lady Elgin and their youngest daughter joined him in January 1863 and the following months were outwardly calm, allowing Lord Elgin time to reflect on the way ahead. The principles of government had been laid down by his predecessors, Dalhousie and Canning, but the role of Secretary of State for India in relation to the Viceroy had still to be defined. The Council of India in London and the legislative council in Calcutta already showed signs of confrontation and the views of dominant figures – for example, John Lawrence of the Punjab, the governor of Bombay, Bartle Frere, and the commander of the army, Sir Hugh Rose – had to be taken into account.

India desperately needed more roads, railways, canals and irrigation, but the country's finances were continuously in deficit. Miss Nightingale's demands for improved army barracks and her new campaign for sanitation and irrigation must have had some impact on the new Viceroy, but there is no record to this effect, other than an oblique reference in Morrison's biography: "Medical and sanitary knowledge, penetrating last of all into army medical circles, was beginning to reveal scandals in the housing of the troops, and the inadequacy of existing barracks."

There is certainly a link through the powerful woman journalist, Harriet Martineau. Florence Nightingale had written to her *"in the joy of my heart"* on the day the Report of the Indian Sanitary Commission was signed – 19 May 1863. Miss Martineau responded by sending articles on the subject of the Report to *The Daily News*, *MacMillan's Magazine*, and *Once a Week*. She also offered to write to her old friends, Lord and Lady Elgin, and the "indefatigable Miss Nightingale" at once sent her the main headings of a letter to go immediately to the Viceroy. But

Lord Elgin had left Calcutta on a fact-finding trip to Benares, Allahabad, Cawnpore, Agra, Delhi, Umballa, and other places, finally reaching Simla for five months' respite in the cool mountain air. Harriet Martineau's letter may never have reached him.

In the autumn the Viceroy and his retinue set out again for Peshawar, their hazardous route taking them at high altitudes to a gorge over the Chandra River. Lord Elgin struggled across a fragile "twig" bridge and subsequently collapsed with a heart attack. He was carried, with great difficulty, to a military station at Dharmsala and, after rallying briefly, died on 30 November 1863. His burial at Dharmsala took place the following day.

Harriet Martineau

Chapter 3

Lord Lawrence (1811–1879)
Viceroy 1864–1868

"The doubts and difficulties of the viceroy were lost in the legend of the man who made the Punjab prosperous and loyal, and who in May 1857 asked a slow-moving commander-in-chief to reflect that since Clive at Plassey the British had not won India by being prudent. 'Where have we failed when we acted vigorously?'"

From private notes and letters it is clear that Florence Nightingale enjoyed her connections with men of power and academic achievement. She was prone to hero-worship, often quoting such disparate figures as Abraham Lincoln, Garibaldi and General Gordon. Benjamin Jowett, her long-time friend and spiritual adviser, observed this facet of her character with wry amusement and would chide her gently from time to time. Not one to take criticism lightly, Florence appeared to accept his admonitions with a meekness that testified to the strength of their relationship.

When John Lawrence strode into Miss Nightingale's quiet house in South Street, Westminster, in March 1861 he was fifty years of age; his administrative work in the Jullundur Doab and the Punjab had been highly praised and, with their shared concern for the welfare of the Indian rural poor, there was much to discuss. Florence Nightingale was the younger by ten years, but the Crimean War had taken a heavy toll; she was in poor health and was receiving few visitors. Her biographer, Sir Edward Cook, describes the aftermath of their talk: "He (Lawrence) found her much better than he expected" – so her cousin Hilary reported – "and said so to Dr Sutherland as he went downstairs. Dr Sutherland replied 'You cannot know, but when I go back I shall find her quite abattue, and shall not speak another word to her.'" But the meeting was undoubtedly a success and marked the beginning of a long, if seemingly improbable, friendship. A photograph of the powerful 1862 portrait of Lawrence by George Frederick Watts dominated Miss Nightingale's bedroom during the last years of her life.

Unlike his fellow Viceroys, John Lawrence could lay no claim to a title or academic honours, nor to a private source of income. He possessed few social graces and dressed carelessly. But he conveyed an impression of decisiveness and power which the Secretary of State Lord Stanley summed up as "a certain heroic simplicity".

John's father, Alexander Lawrence of Coleraine, was

orphaned at an early age and cared for by elder sisters. In his seventeenth year he volunteered for the army and, after four years' service in India, purchased a commission. He survived hairbreadth escapes and severe wounds, but advancement was slow. In 1809 he returned to England and eventually reached the rank of Lieutenant-Colonel. His wife, Catherine, was the daughter of a Donegal clergyman and a descendant of John Knox. They had eight children and were constantly moving from one army post to another; money – or lack of it – was a constant problem. John, their sixth son, was born in Richmond, Yorkshire, in 1811.

The Lawrence way of life was austere and strongly evangelical. After the early death of their eldest son, the next in line, Letitia, became increasingly important as mentor to the children with the help of a much-loved nurse, Margaret. John's lifelong affection and care for both these older women revealed a gentler side to his nature and may go some way to explaining the ease of his relationship with Florence Nightingale.

The demands of army life led to an erratic pattern of education for the Lawrence children. John and his elder brother, Henry, were sent first to Mr Cough's school in Bristol. Henry recalled: "I was flogged every day of my life at school, except one, and then I was flogged twice." John went on to Foyle College in Londonderry where his uncle was headmaster; then to Wrexhall Hall in North Wiltshire, followed by a spell at Clifton where he was nicknamed "Paddy" and kicked for being an Irishman.

He later summed up his progress at this stage: "I worked by fits and starts . . . I was a fair Latin and mathematical scholar and a poor Greek one." It is worth noting, however, that when John, aged twelve, was a pupil at Foyle College, it was recorded that *his historical knowledge, particularly of military campaigns, was remarkable."*

The year 1827 was a turning-point in the affairs of the Lawrence family. A close friend, John Huddlestone, returned to England after holding high office in the Madras Presidency. He secured posts in the Indian Army for the three older brothers – Alexander, George and Henry – but John, to his great disappointment, was offered only an opportunity to study at the East Indian College at Haileybury, leading to a post in the Indian Civil Service. He protested that he would go to India as a soldier, or not at all, but was finally persuaded by his sister. In 1829 he passed out third for a post in the Bengal Presidency and brought home prizes with the comment: "They are Letitia's books . . . I should not have had one of them but for her."

Accompanied by his brother Henry, who had been recovering from a long illness after five years' hard campaigning in India, John sailed round the Cape of Good Hope, surviving seasickness and enduring a hurricane to arrive in Calcutta on 9 February 1830. He completed his foreign language studies at the College of Fort William, passing the necessary examinations in Urdu and Persian. He found the climate enervating and suffered from depression. Social events in the capital held little attraction. He applied for a notoriously difficult

John Lawrence's brother, Henry Lawrence, when resident of Lucknow

post as assistant to the Resident and Chief Commissioner in Delhi, where the natives were known for their warlike character and there was a strong criminal element. The Resident had to keep order, administer justice, apportion and collect land tax and develop the resources of the country. His assistants – four or five in number – lived in the main house or in the compound. They were encouraged to take responsibility for any one of the Resident's functions.

John Lawrence's biographer, R Bosworth Smith, constantly bemoaned the lack of diaries and personal letters during this period and, indeed, throughout Lawrence's life in India. It would seem that much of the material for the first of Bosworth Smith's two volumes of biography stemmed from conversations with the Viceroy after his retirement and the recollections of friends and former colleagues.

John Lawrence's first appointment under the Resident was that of "assistant judge, magistrate and collector of the city and environs, an area of 800 square miles and a population of 500,000 natives of mixed race". He remained in Delhi for four years and was strongly influenced by the "Bengal system" of government which had been developed by Charles Metcalfe in the Delhi area and combined in the person of the Resident the judicial and administrative functions of government. Lawrence then requested a transfer to a particularly difficult district in the northern division of the Delhi territory with a base at Panipat, a town with a history of turbulence. The post did not warrant a European assistant; it was a lonely life, but he had "a good horse and a dog" to keep him company.

Panipat was an acting appointment; after three months Lawrence returned to his former subordinate post in Delhi, but was promoted in 1837 to the grade of "joint magistrate and deputy of the southern division of the Delhi territory". The main towns were Gorgaon and Etawah, each with largely the same racial mix as in the northern territory, but with the added challenge of small gangs of robbers – the Meenas and Mahwattas – who roamed the countryside, pillaging the villages. There were no soldiers stationed in the district, but on the whole crime and violence were kept under reasonable control. Lawrence spent much of the year under canvas; he rode round the district armed and made himself accessible to the people.

Before Lawrence could make progress with his duties as "collector" of land tax, the district had to be surveyed and village boundaries determined by the system devised in 1830 by Lord William Bentinck and his assistant, Robert Bird. Every village exceeding an area of 2,000 square miles was measured, every field mapped, and the nature of the soil recorded; on this basis an assessment of tax was fixed for a period of twenty years. In the event of a dispute a village jury met the British collector, normally under the shade of a convenient tree, and together they would sort out the problem – an informal method of dispensing justice, without pomp or ceremony, that suited Lawrence well. The natives found him formidable: "when he is in anger his voice is like the tiger's roar", but learned to respect and trust this very unusual Englishman.

Etawah (which Lawrence referred to as "a hell hole" in a letter to J Cumine of Rattray, who had spent time with him there) suffered a severe period of drought during the early 1830s, and again in 1837–8, followed by famine. Thousands of Indians left their villages in search of food; many perished and the corpses lay unburied along the roads. Over a period of time Lawrence recalled those terrible scenes of devastation and produced a report in 1845 urging the authorities in Delhi to bring swifter aid to the victims of drought and famine by the provision of better roads and canals and improved communications.

Towards the end of 1839 Lawrence fell seriously ill with jungle fever and was ordered to take a three-year furlough.

Returning to Bristol he found many changes in the family home. Alexander Lawrence had died in 1835; his widow was frail and, unknown to her, totally dependent on a fund set up by her sons. The redoubtable Letitia had married an elderly clergyman, but was still fulfilling her role as head of the household. John had earlier been saddened by the death of their old nurse and now took the opportunity of visiting her grave in a neighbouring county; one of his daughters was named Margaret in her memory.

After two months of convalescence Lawrence was fit enough to make a tour of the Western Highlands with his friend Cumine, followed by a visit to Ireland where he met Harriette, daughter of the Reverend Richard Hamilton in County Meath. John returned to Ireland the following year and, after a short engagement, he and Harriette were married. In a rare fragment of autobiography he wrote: "In 1841 I took perhaps the most important and certainly the happiest step in my life – in getting married. My wife has been everything that a man could hope for."

Their leisurely honeymoon was spent travelling through Belgium, France, Switzerland and Italy. There appears to be no record of their journey or their reactions to the wealth of art, antiquities and architecture that unrolled before their eyes. Letitia and her husband joined them for part of the tour. When news reached them in Naples of an uprising of Afghan tribes against the army, followed by a report that their brother George and his wife had been taken hostage, John wrote a distressed note on 23 March 1842 to Henry's wife Honaria: "I wish I was back in India, all my thoughts and feelings are there. I am heartily tired of Italy . . . Mind and write any particulars which transpire about George. I still live in hope that he may survive."

He and his wife hastened back to England. Once again illness struck and his medical advisers insisted that he should give up all hope of returning to India, to which John responded: "If I can't live in India, I must go and die there."

John and Harriette arrived in Bombay on 14 November 1842 and, after a few days' rest at Government House, set out for the North-West Provinces. A local war had broken out across the direct route and they were forced to make a much longer journey, travelling some three hundred miles through wild, sparsely populated country.

John had been in touch with former colleagues about an administrative post, but so far without success. They faced an unknown future, yet on reaching Allahabad John optimistically invested in tents, two horses and a buggy. Somewhere along the route they met George Lawrence, recently released from captivity by rebel Sikhs and still wearing Afghan garments. He advised John to press on to Delhi and make contact with the Chief Commissioner of the Punjab, Sir Robert Hamilton; then, at last, there followed the offer of an acting appointment at Kurmal. Throughout their long and hazardous journey Harriette had proved remarkably resilient and, now, in this remote military post and in the hottest season of the year, she gave birth to their first daughter, Kate.

John Lawrence spent long hours acquainting himself with the area temporarily under his control. He traced the cause of an epidemic currently affecting both the cantonment and the neighbouring village to the insanitary state of adjoining rice fields where effluent and the carcasses of cattle festered in the sodden earth, and promptly prohibited rice planting within four miles of human habitation. Conditions in the crowded bazaars were another cause for concern and led to a recommendation that they be removed to a safe distance from army barracks. A well-ordered system of sanitary police carrying out regular inspections was essential. A paper produced by Lawrence on these matters came to the notice of Miss Nightingale who pronounced it *"valuable"* and *"life saving"*.

After six months at Kurmal the Lawrence family returned to Delhi for another short-term appointment. A second daughter was born in November 1844. With increasing unrest in the Punjab an experienced soldier, Sir Henry Hardinge, was appointed Governor-General and took command of the army on the outbreak of the First Sikh War. He had met John Lawrence in Delhi and, when in urgent need of guns and ammunition, turned to him for help. Within days Lawrence had requisitioned and despatched 4000 cartloads of supplies, which arrived in time to secure the final victory at Sobraon. His reward followed swiftly when in March 1846 the Governor-General appointed John Lawrence Commissioner of the annexed lands of the Jullundur Doab. At the age of thirty-four Lawrence was at one bound freed from the changes and uncertainties of life as a subordinate administrator.

The territory he now ruled was inhabited by Jats whom

Lawrence described as "a most industrious painstaking race, very quiet and apparently glad to submit to our rule." He offered liberal terms to the ruling Sikh hierarchy, but his avowed aims were to stamp out their ancient abuses and establish the rights of the peasantry.

Lord Hardinge visited John Lawrence's headquarters within a month and found he had no assistants. Two were immediately despatched; one, Lawrence described bluntly as *"fairly useless"*; the other – Robert Cust – became a life-long friend and recalled watching the Commissioner dispense justice: "As each man touched the pen, the unlettered token of agreement to their leases, he made them respect the new dogma of the English Government: 'Thou shalt not burn thy widow; thou shalt not kill thy daughters; thou shalt not bury alive the lepers." 'His rule was stern, but new reforms followed and peace reigned in the Jullundur Doab.

Later in 1846 and again in 1847–8 John was required to deputize for his brother as resident at Lahore due to Henry's need for respite from the stresses of office. Problems in the Punjab were mounting and the assassination of two British officers at Mooltan in April 1848 was followed by the outbreak of full-scale activities and the Second Sikh War. Because of the stable conditions in the Jullundur Doab, Lawrence and his assistants were able to put down insurrections with the use of small mobile forces and the support of locally-raised loyal Sikhs.

With the end of the war and the need to solve settlement problems in the Punjab John Lawrence was forced to spend more time in Lahore, while retaining his post in

Jullundur. He endeavoured to keep the ailing Henry fully informed, but it became increasingly obvious that the brothers were seriously at odds. John disagreed with Henry's sympathy with the ruling Sikh family and finally felt bound to recommend to the new young Governor General, Lord Dalhousie, that the widowed Maharani and her corrupt lover, Lal Sing – currently acting as Regent for the under-age Maharaja – should be removed, and that the Punjab should be governed by the English until the heir attained manhood. The Governor-General agreed, Henry Lawrence was installed as supreme ruler of the Punjab and John was at last free to return to his post.

For the past nine months he had been separated from his family; his eldest son was born in his absence. The Residency lacked comfort; Lawrence, his wife, and now three children occupied two rooms for their private use. Working conditions were also restricted. An assistant, Lewin Bowning, recalled seeing the Commissioner, shirt-sleeves rolled up, a cigar in his mouth, dictating orders to a native scribe who squatted on the floor, while Harriette sat nearby doing her needlework. When a fourth child was born in March 1849 John Lawrence moved his burgeoning family into a house in the cool hill station of Dharmsala.

A board was set up to govern the Punjab chaired by Sir Henry Lawrence with John Lawrence and a third member, who had the delicate task of holding the balance between two brothers with widely differing views: the one concerned to ease the fall of the feudal rulers, the other dedicated to the well-being of the peasantry. Nevertheless there were positive achievements and the board's first report in 1852 to the Directors of the East India Company was described by the Governor-General as "a prosperous result". The Directors were generous in their praise of the members.

But relations between the Lawrence brothers continued to deteriorate and both applied for transfer to another post. Lord Dalhousie, aware of their strengths and weaknesses, offered Sir Henry the Agency to the Governor General in Rajapostana – a task to which he was well suited – and in 1853 appointed John Lawrence Chief Commissioner of the Punjab. Henry was deeply disappointed and embittered. John, saddened by the rift, wrote: "I sincerely wish that you had been left in the Punjab. When I have opposed your views I have done it from a thorough conviction and not from fractious or interested motives. It is more than possible that you and I shall never again meet but I trust all unkindly feeling between us may be forgotten." Sir Henry Lawrence was wounded at Lucknow in 1857 and shortly before his death wrote an acknowledgement of John's help: "without whom I must have had difficulty carrying on". The new Commissioner and his dedicated band of administrators established four years of peace and growing prosperity in the Punjab, freeing the peasants from the abuses of their former rulers and giving them the opportunity to acquire land at a moderate price. Percival Spear gives a lively description of the Punjab system: "The land was settled in favour of the cultivator rather than the chiefs, many of whom John

Lawrence regarded as little better than hereditary bandits. Justice was administered in a rough-and-ready but effective way. The administration was elastic and untiring, with much latitude to the man on the spot and the heavy demands on his energy and devotion. Days were spent in the saddle under a burning sun and nights in writing reports by the light of candles stuck into beer bottles. The gospel of this band was justice and material improvements. Roads, schools, courthouses were the order of the day; engineers would crow over a new bridge as over a newborn infant."

To all the reforms Lord Dalhousie gave his full support and, before his retirement as Governor-General in 1856, secured a knighthood for Lawrence. They continued to correspond in the period leading up to Lord Canning's appointment, but Dalhousie had been suffering from a serious medical condition and died of seasickness on the voyage back to England.

The outbreak of the Indian Mutiny in 1857 marked the second significant turning point in Sir John's life, catapulting him into the role of national hero. He had been surprised – and alarmed – by the speed with which the uprisings at Meerut and Delhi had spread like bush fires across the country; how could the sepoys have been so misled? There were lessons to be learned and Sir John set about raising an army of forty thousand men, with a minimum number of British officers, but he warned General Anson and others that failure to retake Delhi could put the loyalty of the Punjab at risk.

The sombre story of the Indian Mutiny – its seemingly

An engraving of Colonel Campbell's troops storming the Cashmere Gate during the siege of Delhi, 1857

PROCLAMATION
[To the Sepoys in the Punjab]

My advice is that you obey your officers. Seize all those who among yourselves endeavour to mislead you. Let not a few bad men be the cause of your disgrace. If you have the will, you can easily do this and Government will consider it a test of your fidelity. Prove by your conduct that the loyalty of the Hindatsan has not degenerated from that of his ancestors.

JOHN LAWRENCE
Chief Commissioner

trivial causes, the tragic deaths of English men, women and children, and the many acts of heroism – has been told and retold. The first news of the outbreak reached Sir John during the evening of May 12th, followed by a telegram with news of the capture of Delhi and the murder of Europeans. He was suffering from a severe attack of neuralgia; Lady Lawrence recalled that he immediately left his bed and spent the following day assessing the situation. He then sent a stream of letters and telegrams to the Commissioner at Peshawar, the brigadier commanding the Frontier Force, Generals Anson, Barnard and Archdale Wilson, and the Governor-General. Effective communication with his men spread out across the Punjab was difficult, but he relied on their ability to take the necessary decisions and send for help if needed.

Sir John urged the importance of capturing Delhi. His detailed knowledge of the fortifications, which as a young administrator he had helped to strengthen, and his grasp of siege tactics enabled the British besiegers to take the Citadel, leading to the collapse of the Mutiny. Lord Canning withstood a wave of criticism from the Council in London and swiftly restored calm on the Indian continent. With support from Sir John Lawrence and some of the more influential Indian princes, he pursued a firm but lenient policy towards the defeated rebels – hence his nickname "*Clemency Canning*".

Sir John returned to England in 1859, was sworn in as a member of the Privy Council, and awarded a baronetcy with a pension of £2,000 a year from the East

India Company and the new order of the Star of India. He was hailed as saviour of the Indian Empire by press and public alike.

In August 1862 Florence Nightingale completed her *Observations* on reports from stations for inclusion in the Sanitary Commission's Report, seen by many at the time as a unique description of British and native life in India. She paid for copies of the *Observations* to be printed at her own expense and sent them to Lord Stanley, Sir Charles Trevelyan, Sir John McNeill, Sir John Lawrence, and other keen *"Sanitarians"*. A bound copy went to Queen Victoria, who responded with her Collection of Prince Albert's Speeches.

The sudden death in India of the current Viceroy, Lord Elgin, on 30 November 1863 precipitated an urgent search for a successor; Sir John Lawrence's appointment was announced ten days later. Miss Nightingale saw him as *"the indispensable man for India"*; Lord Stanley welcomed *"a great step gained"* for their sanitary reforms, and urged the new Viceroy to call at South Street before sailing for India. In a letter to Sir Harry Verney thirty years later Florence Nightingale recalled the interview as *"one never to be forgotten"*. Sir John asked her to formulate proposals for a drainage system and a course of action that could be used by the Army Sanitary Committee (reinforced by India Office representatives) in negotiations with the Indian government.

Within a month of his arrival in Calcutta Sir John Lawrence confirmed that sanitary committees for Calcutta, Madras and Bombay had been set up and asked Miss Nightingale to send urgently "an idea of the main features of the sanitary system which could be readily adopted to the peculiar circumstances of the country".

By January 1864 Florence Nightingale, working closely with experts, had produced *Suggestions for Improving Indian Stations* for the Barrack and Hospital Improvement Commission, together with a draft submission to the India Office, but to her increasing frustration seven months passed without acknowledgement of any significant action. Sir Edward Cook in his biography recounts the sorry, and sometimes hilarious, tale of missing papers, the stand-off between the War Office and the India Office, Miss Nightingale's machinations, and the final breakthrough by Lord Stanley, leading to the speedy adoption of the proposals (with minor alterations).

Florence then moved swiftly. On 8 August 1864 she wrote to Captain Galton at the War Office: *"I beg to inform you that by the first mail after signature I sent off by H.M.'s book-post at an enormous expense (I have a good mind to charge it to you!) to Sir John Lawrence direct no end of Suggestions (also to the Presidency Commissions) and that he is always more than ready to hear than you are to pray (you sinners!), I have not the least doubt that they will be put in execution long before the India Office has even begun to send them."* It was, indeed, six to seven weeks before the official copies were sent to India. There progress was rapid; Sir John kept Miss Nightingale informed of every step taken, either personally or through his Personal Secretary, Dr Hathaway. An amusing comment made at the time by Sir Bartle Frere, Governor of Bombay, is quoted by Cook: "Men used to say that when the Viceroy had received a letter from Miss Nightingale it was like the ringing of a bell to call for sanitary progress."

Their correspondence continued throughout Sir John's viceroyalty. In an early letter Miss Nightingale wrote: *"My dear Sir John Lawrence – I always feel it a kind of presumption in me to write to you – and a kind of wonder at your permitting it."* For his part, Sir John wrote (probably late at night) not on official notepaper but seemingly on whatever came to hand, using both sides of the sheets. He described his journeys through the country, the conditions he found in military stations, and his problems with the India Council in London. In return Florence Nightingale's letters covered an extraordinary range of subjects: the state of police hospitals in Calcutta, conditions in Indian jails and lunatic asylums and the need for decent sailors' homes in the main ports, along with news of his children in England, which Sir John acknowledged gratefully on 3 December 1863: "It was truly kind of you to write and give me so nice an account of my children at Southgate; it was indeed a very pleasant one and brought them vividly back to my memory. I am sure they are all happier and better in that comfortable old house and English home, than out here. I only wish I could persuade my wife of this and induce her to remain with them." Lady Lawrence, however, won the argument, as confirmed in Miss Nightingale's note to Sir John in December 1864: *"I rejoice to think that, by this time, Lady Lawrence and your daughters are with you."*

It is clear from their correspondence in the ensuing years that Sir John Lawrence found viceregal life increasingly difficult, becoming wearied and depressed by the pressure of demands on his time, and the chronic lack of funding to carry through essential public works and sanitary reforms. Miss Nightingale refrained from criticism, praising what had been achieved in an effort to raise his flagging spirits, but Sir John felt himself unworthy of her commendations. He wrote in February 1865: "All that I really do is try and help you when I think your plans and propositions are feasible", ending with the sad words: "I am afraid you will consider me timid and time-serving." But Florence Nightingale remained unswerving in her loyalty to Sir John, writing to her confidante in Paris, Madame Mohl: *"Certainly Sir J. Lawrence is the only man who ever called Sir J. Lawrence a time-server − except in the highest possible sense of serving his country at her time of greatest need."*

As the years passed it became clear that the Viceroy no longer had the stamina for political infighting, passing Miss Nightingale's letters to others to answer, and confessing in a note to her dated 16 August 1867: "I am not well and have more on my hands than I can manage . . . We have so little money in India and so much to do". Florence Nightingale would have recognised the signs of battle weariness, bearing in mind her affection for the Crimean War veterans with whom she remained in touch, writing to them towards the end of her active life (26 October 1897): *"My Dear Old Comrades − I think of you on Balaclava Day and many days besides"*, and exhorting them to be thankful for *"the last years of our lives which ought to be the best years of our lives."*

John Lawrence, created Baron Lawrence of the Punjab and Grateley (a small estate on Salisbury Plain left him by his sister Letitia), retired as Viceroy in January 1869, having passed the baton – with huge relief – to Lord Mayo. Lady Lawrence was awarded the Star of India. Both as wife to the Commissioner of the Punjab, and as Vicereine, Harriette had shown extraordinary courage and adaptability; she nursed her husband through fevers, acted at times as his secretary, established makeshift homes in unlikely settings, and gave birth to ten children under far from ideal conditions, faced with the knowledge that she must be separated from them during their formative years.

At the time of the Mooltan uprising Harriette received an urgent message from her husband that she should make her way, with four children and an English nurse-maid, to the hill fort of Kanga, twelve miles away. The small group travelled in jampans, a chair carried on the bearers' shoulders, or on their heads when crossing streams. The fortitude shown by this young woman from a quiet Irish rectory is truly remarkable; but it should also be remembered that many other wives of Indian administrators endured similar hardships during the Raj years.

On their return to London, Lord and Lady Lawrence set up residence at 23 Queen's Gate Gardens, South Kensington. Lord Lawrence made an early call at South Street, first leaving a note and "a small shawl of the fine hair of the Thibet goat", perhaps testing his reception, but there was no need. In a long note describing their meeting on 3 April 1869 Miss Nightingale wrote:

". . . when I see him again I see there is no-one like him . . . he has left his mark on India."

In spite of poor health and failing eyesight, Lord Lawrence worked long hours for the London Education Board: he found it exhausting. With the help of a Private Secretary (*"female"* commented Miss Nightingale – a twinge of jealousy perhaps?) he read Parliamentary Blue Books and kept abreast of Indian politics. In his last speech in Parliament, just a week before his death on 27 June 1879, he spoke on the Indian finance problem and deplored the increase in taxation.

Despite politically motivated objections from Lord Beaconsfield, Mr Gladstone authorized Lord Lawrence's burial in Westminster Abbey and attended the funeral on 6 July 1879. The following day Miss Nightingale wrote to the Prime Minister with her memories of John Lawrence's last days: *"He was a man of iron; he had gone thro' 40 years of Indian life, in times of danger, toil and crisis; had been brought seven times to the brink of the grave; and had weathered it all – to die of a School Board at last!"* (Throughout her writings Florence Nightingale had this extraordinary ability to cut through emotional outbursts with shafts of ironic humour – perhaps to steady herself?) The day after Lord Lawrence's death she received her final letter from him, enclosing recent Indian reports with passages marked for her attention; it had been dictated, but signed by him.

A much-quoted summing-up of Lord Lawrence's vice-regal years is to the effect that had he ruled India as he ruled the Punjab he would have been hailed as a brilliant

caricature of Lord Lawrence

viceroy. There were, however, positive achievements: the judicial system was reformed, forestry departments created, the railways extended, and an improved standard of education encouraged for the children of the rising Indian middle classes. Level-headed, as always, in military matters, Lord Lawrence pursued a policy of what he saw as masterly inactivity in the regions bordering India's frontiers.

The question of army sanitation in India had seemed to officials in the War Office to be just one out of a vast number of problems confronting them; to Miss Nightingale it was *"a matter of life or death"* and it was widely acknowledged that her passionate conviction was the driving force for reform. But Sir Edward Cook – her fair-minded biographer – pays tribute to Lord Lawrence's contribution: "Sir John had much else on his mind other than the promotion of sanitary improvements for the Army in India, but his promotion of that work as a Viceroy whose heart and soul were in it made all the difference. If the Viceroy had been hostile or apathetic Florence Nightingale's persistence might have been foiled. Their co-operation was vital."

Chapter 4

Richard Southwell Bourke, Lord Mayo (1822–1872)
Viceroy 1869–1872

". . . had seen more of India in his three years [before assassina-
tion] than most civil servants managed in a lifetime and knew more
about India than any other viceroy until George Curzon at the end
of the century."

The Sixth Earl of Mayo was widely regarded as one
of the most successful and beloved of viceroys up to the
end of the nineteenth century. Florence Nightingale
remembered him warmly:
"I think he was the most open man, except Sidney Herbert, I
ever knew". But any study of his career must be over-
shadowed with the awareness that his life was cut short
by the pointless blow of a crazed native while on a visit
to the Andaman Islands, a cruel stroke of fate which
reverberates in the mind.

Richard Southwell Bourke (1822–72) came from an Irish background. His father, Robert, was brother and heir to the Hon. Richard Bourke, the Fourth Earl of Mayo and Bishop of Waterford. A biography of Richard, the Sixth Earl, published in 1875 by W W Hunter of the Bengal Civil Service describes a happy family life in their relatively unpretentious home, "Hayes" in County Meath. Richard, the eldest of eight children, was educated by his father and much influenced in spiritual matters by his mother, Anne. Apparently not a scholar by nature, apart from an interest in history, he preferred outdoor pursuits in which he excelled.

From 1838 to 1840 the family settled in Paris, with the benefits of a French tutor and governess, but much of this period was devoted to a walking tour in the Bernese Oberland followed by a winter in Florence. Richard and his brother, John, were of an age to attend balls and other entertainments. Richard fell in love and wrote verses to his beloved about whom, discreetly, nothing is known.

Entry to Trinity College, Dublin, in 1841 led to a modest degree. He chose not to reside in college, preferring to stay with his great-uncle, the Fourth Earl, and his lively wife. Their home, "Palmerston", was a hospitable house and it was there that Richard learned to be at ease in sophisticated society. He also spent time in London enjoying the social life and discussing English politics with Conservative friends – described at the time as: "A very young man, with a fine bearing, one of the best waltzers in town and a great deal made of". A journey with a

e Viceroy Lord Mayo in his Star of India robes

friend to Russia in 1845 led to Richard's published account of their travels in two volumes – *St. Petersburg and Moscow: a Visit to the Court of the Czar* – with realistic descriptions of the Russian peasants and village life. As a member of a liberal-minded family which believed in the responsibilities attached to the ownership of property, he was deeply distressed by the painful evidence of "serf-life" and commented on the absence of a middle class which he saw as "the necessary cement of a social state".

Meanwhile Ireland was suffering from the effects of potato blight, followed by years of famine. It was a terrible time for landowners, particularly those of moderate means. Richard "lived in the saddle", attending public meetings, arranging for the distribution of charitable funds and food supplies to outlying communities. In flying visits to England he sold shawls and other products from the cottagers and took part in dramatic performances for charity. His father gave him a small farm on the family estate; he drained and improved the land, bought cattle and studied the principles of agriculture and stockbreeding. In a note Florence Nightingale wrote after Lord Mayo's death, she recalled his saying that his Irish experience was so useful to him in India and that he was "*. . . certainly the only Viceroy who had sold his cattle in the market*".

Richard was elected Conservative Member of Parliament for Kildare in 1847 (later representing Coleraine and Cockermouth). He was known for his liberal views, which endeared him to his Irish constituents, and was a regular attender of debates. In 1848 he married Blanche

Wyndham, daughter of the first Lord Leconfield. There were four sons and three daughters of the marriage, from all accounts a very happy union. During their viceregal years Lady Mayo returned to England to spend a few months with the children and received a letter from her husband with the endearing message "we have never been separated before for any length of time. I hope you will dislike it." When in 1849 his father succeeded to the earldom, Richard assumed the courtesy title of Lord Nash and duly made his maiden speech in the House of Lords. He wrote to his mother: "Disraeli and others told me I did capitally. I was, as you may imagine, in a blue funk." During the years that followed Liberals and Conservatives moved in and out of power with bewildering rapidity. In 1852, after a period in the wilderness, the Conservatives returned under Lord Derby and Lord Nash was brought into the Cabinet as Chief Secretary for Ireland, an office he continued to hold with quiet efficiency in subsequent administrations. In 1876, on the death of his father, he succeeded to the Mayo earldom and in the same year Disraeli (now Lord Beaconsfield) put forward his name as fourth Viceroy of India. At this point the Conservative government fell. Mr Gladstone considered revoking the appointment but, on reflection, allowed the offer to stand.

Mayo had welcomed the challenge with huge enthusiasm. There had been an outcry about the appointment in the Liberal press equally critical of the Conservative Party and Mayo himself, who was little known – but throughout this difficult period he had the steadfast support of Lord Beaconsfield. In the weeks before his departure for India he made many useful contacts, dined with the Prince of Wales at Windsor, and spent long hours in the India Office discussing irrigation, railways and finance; he was said to the best briefed of all the Viceroys up to the time of Curzon. But he left England with no preconceived ideas, preferring to judge conditions as he found them.

One of his advisers was Sir Bartle Frere, a former Governor of Bombay and, in retirement, a member of the Indian Council in London. Frere urged him to call on Miss Nightingale with whom he had corresponded on their common concerns for improved public works for the Indian people, particularly in the areas of sanitation and irrigation. He wrote to one of his children from Bombay: "You ask why I am always thinking and talking of irrigation. If you had seen men's bones, as I have, lying unburied by the roadside, and on entering a village had found it untenanted by a living person, you would understand why."

Miss Nightingale saw Lord Mayo on 28 October 1868 and Lady Mayo a few days later. The meeting was a success. In a note to Dr Sutherland she reported their conversation: *"What he said was not unsensible but essentially Irish . . . he asked me (over and over again) that I now at once before he goes write down for him something (he said) 'that would guide me upon the sanitary administration as soon as I arrive . . . especially about that Executive. He asked most sagacious questions about all the men."* In consultation with Sir Bartle Frere and Dr Sutherland she wrote a Memorandum for the new Viceroy covering the whole ground of sanitary improvement and dwelling on the need for irrigation and agricultural development.

On 11 November 1868 Lord Mayo crossed the Channel and continued by train from Paris to the Italian port of Brindisi where his party boarded Her Majesty's Ship *Psyche* for the voyage to Alexandria – a total journey of twenty-six days. His biographer, William Hunter, had access to Mayo's diary which reveals something about the man who would become Viceroy: his stamina, thirst for knowledge, and ability to relate to people at all levels. Hunter comments that the entries *"contained not one unkind word"* and little about his family life which, throughout his career, he kept rigorously separate from public scrutiny.

After six days at sea *Psyche* arrived at Alexandria (then part of the Ottoman Empire) and Lord Mayo was received *"with great civility"* by the Turkish Viceroy. The existence of his harem is noted without any further comment. Lord Napier of Magdala, Commander-in-Chief of the Army in India, had come to greet and escort the incoming Viceroy. A visit to the Pyramids by Nile steamer was arranged and on by rail to Ismailia where, at a reception hosted by the French, Mayo met the brilliant engineer, Ferdinand de Lesseps. Together they studied plans and working drawings for the vast Suez Canal project, due for completion by 1870. (It was opened in 1869.) A visit to the site followed; then to Port Said, a city of twenty thousand people created by the Suez Canal Company. Mayo found the French organisation of the project very impressive and made copious notes in his diary covering "two of the most interesting days I have ever spent in my life". For the first time he mentions Lady Mayo's presence at a dinner given by their French friends.

The week-long voyage from Suez across the Indian Ocean provided a welcome respite; there were no entries in the diary. On 8 December they reached Aden, the first outpost of the Indian Empire. Here Mayo is sharply critical of the military defences and marks the need for a railway from the Isthmus to Steamer Point to serve the increased traffic that would pass through the Canal, and for an improved water supply for the growing population of the port. After a few more peaceful days at sea their ship reached Bombay early on Sunday 20 December 1868. There was a band and a guard of honour on the dock and the party drove by carriage to Government House where they were received by the Governor-General, Sir Seymour Fitzgerald.

The following day Mayo rode out early to see the discharge from one of the main sewers. He had already checked that "Our horses have arrived and, considering the voyage, are looking remarkably well." At an evening reception he was presented to "an immense number of people", among them the Rájá of Jamkhandi, who brought his wife ". . . a nice little woman who speaks some English. He is much wondered at and abused by the natives for taking his wife into society". In a later diary entry he describes an elaborate ceremony to welcome the Chief of Porbandar and his two sons: "The ceremony of reception, which I believe is the same on all similar occasions, is this: the Chief and his two sons, who were covered in jewels, were led in by an ADC. Fitzgerald and I were seated on a sofa at the end of a long room. The Rájá was invited to sit down beside us, and after a few commonplace sentences, a gold box, a cup, and a bottle of scent were brought. Powder and otto of roses were sprinkled by Fitzgerald on the Rájá's pocket handkerchief, the same thing being done by the aide-de-camp to the two sons. A large garland of flowers was then brought in on a tray. This garland Fitzgerald placed round the Rájá's neck, with a garland for each of his arms, and a huge bouquet. The same was done for each of his sons. The whole ceremony did not last more than six or seven minutes. This followed by a dinner party of eighty." Mayo was fast learning the shape of things to come.

The restless round of activities continued over a period of eight days in Madras, where his host was the Governor. Lord Napier of Ettrick. There were stately functions, lavish meals and long discussions with key officials, combined with expeditions to inspect army barracks, a new hospital and college, and a voyage by steamer round the commercial port of Madras to assess naval and military works – all this in the searing Indian heat and dust. Even a man of Mayo's robust constitution must have found it hard to adapt. Three of his predecessors, Canning, Elgin and Dalhousie (a former Governor-General) had either died in office or shortly after their return to England. Then back at sea he writes on 8 January 1869: "Paid the penalty of my imprudence and over-exertion at Madras, being attacked sharply by fever." Three days later he reports: "better but still very weak".

Government House, Madras

The Esplanade, Calcutta, at the time of Lord Mayo's arrival in India

The official reception at Calcutta had to be faced the following day.

The ship berthed at 4.30 in the afternoon of Tuesday 12 January 1869. Immense crowds had gathered. Lord Mayo was received by Sir John Lawrence and members of the Council of India and duly sworn in as Viceroy of India.

That same evening, at a state dinner given by Lord Lawrence, the new Viceroy in his viceregal uniform was reported to look "the picture of radiant health". Senior officials present had read the bitter attacks in the English press, but were disarmed by his ease of manner and general air of well-being. Here, they felt, was a man of stature who could handle a punishing workload and stand up to the rigours of the Indian climate.

Lord Mayo's stamina was remarkable. During three years in office it is recorded that he travelled 21,763 miles using a strange variety of conveyances, from river steamer and hand-operated trolleys on half-finished rail tracks, to camels, elephants, yaks and inflated buffalo skins on the River Indus, doubtless taking every experience in his stride and relishing his new freedom.

But first he must master the mechanism of the Supreme Government of India, described in succinct terms by Miss Nightingale: *'that Council . . . those men".* The Council had been remodelled by Lord Canning into the semblance of a Cabinet with the Governor-General as President, subject to the authority of the Secretary of State in London, and in direct control of the twelve Provincial Governments and 153 Native States. Papers on matters for discussion in Council were passed *"at a snail's pace"* in small mahogany boxes from one member to another. Minutes of meetings were handwritten in lengthy and elaborate style, with copies to the Secretary of State. Each member had responsibility for a Department. The Governor-General kept one Department in his hands, usually Foreign Affairs, but Lord Mayo claimed both Foreign Affairs and Public Works. His decision to monitor progress on roads and railways, canals, irrigation and drainage projects, may well have been prompted by his talks with Florence Nightingale and their exchange of letters, which continued throughout his viceroyalty. Certainly there are echoes of her insistent voice in Lord Mayo's speech to the assembled Princes and Chiefs of Rájputâna at a darbar at Ajmir: "I, as representative of the Queen, have come here to tell you, as you have often been told before, that the desire of Her Majesty's Government is to secure to you and to your successors the full enjoyment of your ancient rights and the exercise of all lawful customs, and to assist you in upholding the dignity and maintaining the authority which you and your fathers have for centuries exercised in this land. But in order to enable us fully to carry into effect this our fixed resolve, we must receive from you hearty and cordial assistance. If we respect your rights and privileges, you should respect the rights and privileges of those who are placed beneath your care. If we support you in your power, we expect in return good government. We demand that everywhere, throughout the length and breadth of Rãjputáná, justice and order shall be secure; that the traveller shall come and go in safety; that the cultivator shall enjoy the fruits of his labour and the trader the produce of his commerce; that you shall make roads, and undertake the construction of those works of irrigation which will improve the condition of the people and swell the revenues of your States; that you shall encourage education and provide for the relief of the sick . . ."

After this speech one of Lord Mayo's Councillors wrote: "Every Native Prince who met him looked upon Lord Mayo as the ideal of an English Viceroy . . . while they knew he was their master, they felt also that he was their friend." In foreign affairs the Viceroy was equally successful subduing the unruly Afghans and sending his personal emissary to Moscow to secure an assurance from the Tsar that there would be no Russian encroachment on Indian territory. With the help of his able Private Secretary and Foreign Affairs Secretary his working day was tightly planned, beginning with paperwork at daybreak when the air was cool, followed by meetings with local officials and foreign envoys; then a round of visits which might involve laying a foundation stone, inspection of works in progress on a new railway or canal, or giving a speech as Chancellor of Calcutta University. In the late afternoon he would usually find time for a refreshing gallop and half-an-hour of story-telling with his youngest son. Dinner followed at 8.30, with various entertainments which seldom ended before midnight.

In spite of the pressures, Lord Mayo still kept up with personal correspondence. On 1 February 1870 he wrote a reassuring note to the father of a young man who was staying at Government House and helping the viceregal aides. Lord Mayo regrets he could not spend time with him because he was "overwhelmed with work" and with "forty-two people staying in my house". In a more cheerful frame of mind he describes in a report dated 15 March 1870 to the Duke of Argyll a week spent on horseback: "I had a most interesting tour through the Coal and Cotton districts of Chandra and the Benars. Opened the little State Railway at Khargarence. Came on and met the Duke of Edinburgh at Jubblepore."

Despite almost daily battles on funding between London and the Indian Council, Lord Mayo working with Sir Richard Temple (Finance Minister) and Sir John Strachey (Home Minister), succeeded in overturning a crippling deficit and establishing a realistic financial policy. Re-organisation of the wasteful Public Works Department enabled essential projects to go forward. Extension of the railways brought swifter relief to famine-stricken areas and opened up trading opportunities; Lord Mayo insisted that third class passengers must be able to travel in reasonable comfort. Skilled engineers began work on major irriga-tion and sanitation projects, and a timetable for improve-ments to army barracks was drawn up, again using experienced engineers. There were more plans in the pipeline, including a Census and Statistical Survey of India, but for Lord Mayo time was running out . . .

On 26 January 1872 the Viceroy and Lady Mayo boarded Her Majesty's Frigate *Glasgow* – together with a party of distinguished guests on a second ship – and sailed for the Andaman Islands, refounded as a convict colony in 1858.

A cover of the *Graphic* depicts scenes from the Andaman Islands

With a mere handful of soldiers guarding 8,000 convicts there had been a spiralling lack of discipline. New controls and an overhaul of prison buildings were needed.

From the point of disembarkation at Hopetown on 8 February strict security measures were observed. The only convicts quartered in the area were "ticket-of-leave" men of approved good conduct. After a strenuous tour of inspection the indefatigable Lord Mayo proposed that, with an hour of daylight left, they should climb to the summit of Mount Harriet to view a possible site for a sanitorium for fever patients. It was a stiff climb and after inspection Lord Mayo sat down to watch the sun setting over the sea: "How beautiful" he was heard to murmur.

Dusk had fallen and the group descended through the jungle in close formation. On the quay torchbearers came to meet them and escort the Viceroy to the waiting launch. As he stepped forward a tall figure rushed from behind a pile of stones, leapt upon his back and stabbed him twice with great force. Men rushed to seize the aggressor. Lord Mayo stumbled into the water but managed to rise, saying quietly to his Private Secretary: "Burne, they've hit me", then in a louder voice to reassure those on the quayside: "I don't think I am much hurt", but he was mortally wounded and died before reaching the ship where Lady Mayo had been waiting on deck to welcome him.

The assassin, Sher Ali, was a Pathan who had served in the Punjab mounted police and had been condemned to death for slaying a man. But the evidence was unclear and the sentence was commuted to life imprisonment on the Andamans, where he behaved well and was eventually given "ticket-of-leave" status. He confessed to the crime, saying that he had waited patiently for a chance to kill a European of high rank, believing it was God's will. After a trial Sher Ali was condemned to death by hanging. The last message he received was from Lady Mayo and her family: "God forgive you as we do"

The Viceroy's body was brought back to Calcutta and borne through grieving crowds to lie in state for two days in Government House. Before leaving for India Lord Mayo had visited the family burial-ground, a simple country churchyard on his Kildare estate and expressed a wish to be buried there – and in that peaceful place he was laid to rest, his grave marked by a stone Celtic cross.

The English and Indian newspapers published moving tributes to a remarkable Viceroy. Even the fractured Irish nation joined wholeheartedly in praising its famous son. Miss Nightingale privately mourned the loss of a friend and staunch ally.

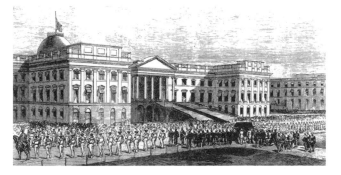

The procession bearing Lord Mayo's coffin arrives at Government House, Calcutta

Chapter 5

Thomas George Baring, Lord Northbrook (1826–1904)
Viceroy 1872–76

". . . not a masterful viceroy but a competent administrator with clear ideas about what was desirable and possible . . . Official India respected him: educated Indians, to whom the future belonged, believed he was their best friend."

Lord Northbrook was a prudent man, as befitted a descendant of the Baring dynasty. Over the course of two centuries in their roles as merchants and bankers, members of the family amassed considerable fortunes, married advantageously, invested in property and became increasingly eminent in public life. Lord Northbrook's vice regal career reflected their prudence in his handling of financial matters – but without their flair – and combined this with meticulous attention to detail and a stubborn aversion to change. But he steered a steady course throughout his term of office, bringing a welcome sense of stability in the aftermath of the Mutiny.

The Barings' English connection stems from a pastor in Bremen whose grandson Johann (John) was despatched to Exeter in 1717 as an apprentice in the cloth trade. He rose rapidly in a firm which handled production of a special type of cloth, eventually acquiring a major share in the business, and married the daughter of a wealthy citizen of Exeter, Elizabeth Vowler – seemingly a remarkable woman who helped John with the management of his affairs. They left comfortable legacies to their five children. The eldest, Francis, had a brilliant career in the City of London, culminating in 1793 in a baronetcy conferred by the Prime Minister, William Pitt the Younger, for his chairmanship of the East India Company.

Young Thomas Baring's father, Sir Thomas Thornhlll Baring, was the second son of Sir Francis, succeeding to the baronetcy in 1845 after the death of his elder brother. He studied law at Christ Church, Oxford, gaining a double first, and entered Parliament as a Whig supporter in 1826. Thomas was thirteen years of age when his father was appointed Chancellor of the Exchequer and twenty-three when he became First Lord of the Admiralty – a hard act to follow. The mother, sister of Sir George Grey – an influential figure in Whig politics – is described as *"high-minded"* in her son's biography. Her death at the age of thirty-four left a grieving father with three young children. At the time the family was described by a guest as a disciplined household with the emphasis on moral and religious training and set periods for bible reading and prayer.

For reasons which are not entirely clear, Sir Francis, a Wykehamist, decided that Thomas should be privately educated. From all accounts he was reserved and studious, encouraged by his father to "acquire knowledge for its own sake; his last tutor judged him to be of a general intelligence and knowledge considerably above the common run of his age".

Entry to Christ Church, Oxford, in 1843 as a gentleman commoner opened windows to a wider life. As was usual with the sons of wealthy families, he brought with him a manservant and a horse for hunting. He became known for his good sportsmanship and high spirits, making friends who would remain close all his life. They spent the long vacations in Europe and, encouraged by the artist Edward Lear, Thomas developed his interest in art and a gift for sketching in pen and watercolour which he used to good effect during his time in India. Inevitably, his studies suffered, but after two years of this congenial life he wrote to his father promising to do better; "I have begun today to read from nine to twelve in the evening, quite a novelty for me at Oxford." He left with a creditable degree in classics.

Marriage at the early age of twenty-four to Elizabeth Sturt, the sister of two Oxford friends, together with entry into the political field, brought growing pressures. The marriage would seem to have been happy, but it is disconcerting to learn that he was reading Dante's works at the time of the birth of his first child in Florence and writing a lengthy dissertation on Venetian art to an Oxford friend.

Thomas Baring's political career began with unpaid posts as Private Secretary to a series of ministers – all his relations – in a variety of government departments. In 1857 he was elected Whig member for Penryn and Falmouth at the second attempt and subsequently held minor posts in the Admiralty and India Office.

When Gladstone suggested that he become Viceroy of India, following the assassination of Lord Mayo, his first instinct was to refuse: "No ambition for (the) office or feeling that I could do good in it." Under pressure he agreed, but still had reservations.

Unlike his predecessors, the Lords Lawrence and Mayo, the new Viceroy neither called nor wrote to Miss Nightingale before sailing for India. In mitigation he was forced to leave at a month's notice following the tragic death of Lord Mayo and spent the available time in Hampshire with his children and close friends. Florence was hurt; they were acquainted and he had been a friend and colleague of Sidney Herbert, so would have been well aware of the extent of their work for the army in India. She made her feelings known to her good friend Benjamin Jowett, who wrote soothingly, or perhaps reprovingly: "Put not your trust in princes or princesses or in the War Office or in the India Office; all that sort of thing necessarily rests on a sandy foundation."

Time passed. There was no communication from India.

Then on 21 July 1874 Lord Napier of Magdala, Commander-in-Chief of the Army in India, reported to Florence that much-needed improvements to army barracks were being delayed year after year: ". . . I cannot help telling you, dear Miss Nightingale, as I know you love the soldiers as well as you did in the Crimea when you broke down the doors of red tape for them . . ."

In consultation with Sir Bartle Frere and Dr Sutherland, she prepared a statement of outstanding works [Appendix] and despatched it in October 1874 to Lord Salisbury, now back for a second term as Secretary of State in the India Office. Lord Salisbury immediately wrote to the Viceroy: "I send you a letter from Miss

Lord Northbrook seated between his daughter Emma and his cousin Evelyn Baring, later the Governor of Egypt

Nightingale. I should be glad to give her a satisfactory answer and therefore hope you will let your Private Secretary note down what you have done or have resolved to do in any of the cases she names on which a resolution has been framed." Predictably, Lord Northbrook's reply dated 11 December claimed that lack of funds was the main reason for the delay in carrying out the necessary improvements, ending with the words: "I can promise you that, so far as our funds permit, every attention shall be paid to the health of the British and Native Army in India." In a courteous acknowledgement Lord Salisbury comments: "I am afraid the writing of it must have been a serious addition to your labours . . . but Miss Nightingale fully deserves the exertion." An excellent illustration of the civilised manner in which affairs of state were conducted in the nineteenth century.

Regrettably, the tone of correspondence between London and Calcutta continued to cause dissension. Both men had genuine concern for the welfare of the Indian people and could, in certain areas, work well together; for example in a review of famine doctrine in 1873. But Northbrook failed to appreciate Lord Salisbury's high-spirited and sometimes visionary approach to Indian problems and criticized his style. By contrast, his own reports grew steadily longer, duller and more autocratic, summed up by the historian, Percival Spear, as: ". . . governing with rigour the most colourful of lands with the most colourless of letters".

Lord Northbrook's advisers were unhelpful and friendly

warnings went unheeded. Finally, in January 1876, he announced his resignation *"for family reasons"* (his son had formed an unsuitable attachment in India), but there were rumours that he felt bullied by Lord Salisbury. Return to England was marked by the customary earldom, appointment as First Lord of the Admiralty in 1880, and an official mission to Egypt in 1884 – after that a long retirement at the family home, Stratton, in Hampshire, emerging from time to time to proffer advice to succeeding Viceroys.

On 3 January 1873 Lord Northbrook had written to Miss Nightingale in response to a letter asking him to receive the civil and sanitary engineer, Mr W Clark, reporting that he had seen the engineer and visited the irrigation works at the Salt Lakes. He went on in friendly fashion assuring her that he knew the importance of pure water and concluding: "I shall always receive with pleasure and consider with attention any suggestions you may kindly give me." Florence did not reply – perhaps the words rang hollow.

Chapter 6

Edward Robert Bulwer Lytton
First Earl of Lytton (1831–91)
Viceroy 1876–81

" Lytton's term of office was one of the most turbulent in viceregal history . . . the long-term effects of the establishment of the new famine code were undoubtedly beneficial and mark the most significant – and perhaps the only – achievement of Lytton's viceroyalty."

Robert Lytton is not an easy man to define; throughout his life he was, and remains, an enigma. He had a brilliant mind, literary talent and great charm, but his career as Viceroy was marred by mood swings and perverse indulgence in unseemly behaviour. Reports in the English and Indian press of scandals connected with the viceregal entourage obscured the positive achievements of his years in India.

Lytton was born in 1831, the only son of the first Baron Bulwer Lytton, politician and writer, best remembered as the author of *The Last Days of Pompeii*. The father's turbulent marriage with a beautiful, but neurotic, Irish girl was dissolved in a long-running saga of legal wrangles. Robert, aged five, was placed in the care of a female relative. He was privately educated at first, then sent to Harrow school, finishing with a modern language course at Bonn on the Rhine. During these formative years he had no contact with his mother and received only occasional visits from the father he revered.

Robert developed a precocious literary talent; he dreamed of devoting his life to poetry. His first volume of romantic verse, with the fetching title *Clytemnestra, The Earl's Return and Other Poems*, was published in 1855, followed by *The Wanderer* in 1857. Both were written – at his father's urging – under the pseudonym Owen Meredith, and were reviewed with mild praise in *The Spectator* and the *Edinburgh Review*, giving him an entrée to London literary circles.

During the 1850s Robert Lytton embarked on a career in the diplomatic service, first as unpaid private secretary to his uncle, Baron Dallinger, the British Ambassador at Washington and later with him in Florence, then in a steady progression of paid posts at embassies across Europe: The Hague, Vienna, Belgrade, Copenhagen, Athens, Madrid and Paris (his favourite city). Lytton had always been something of a dandy, as befitted a poet, but now adopted a Continental way of life and manner

– for example, kissing a lady's hand by way of greeting and dressing in Bohemian style. He lacked height, but was undoubtedly attractive, with sparkling blue eyes, an impressive beard, and the air of a romantic dreamer, vaguely reminiscent of the Pre-Raphaelite Brotherhood who flourished in England in the mid-nineteenth century.

In 1864 Lytton married the beautiful and well-connected Edith Villiers, and on the death of his father in January 1876 (much lamented by him in verse and prose), inherited the title and family estate, Knebworth in Hertfordshire. An appointment as Minister of Legation at Lisbon followed: an agreeable post, well suited to his increasingly hedonistic temperament, with freedom to develop his literary and theatrical interests. An offer in 1875 of the governorship of Madras had been declined on health grounds. Lytton had suffered for some years from a painful malady (subsequently revealed as haemorrhoids) and it was feared that the Indian climate would exacerbate the condition.

At the age of forty-four Lytton was, in fact, planning to retire from the diplomatic service and settle down with his family at Knebworth, devoting his time to improvement of the estate and the *"pursuit of literature"*. But a letter dated 23 November 1875 from Disraeli offering him the viceroyship – following the resignation of Lord Northbrook – put an end to this dream. Lytton hesitated, referring again to health problems and his lack of knowledge of Indian affairs, *"knowing nothing of India except its myths"*. Disraeli overruled his objections and the appointment was announced. It caused some surprise in political circles, but Queen Victoria gave it her blessing. The Lytton family sailed for India on 20 March 1876.

Florence Nightingale had been disheartened by Lord Northbrook's lack of progress with sanitary reform in India. She was unacquainted with Lord Lytto and made no attempt to approach him. Contact with the Prime Minister was the obvious route, but although Claydon House in Buckinghamshire – the home of her brother-in-law, Sir Harry Verney – was only a few miles from Disraeli's house at Hughenden, the two households had little in common. The Verneys were staunch Liberals. It so happened that three years later Miss Nightingale pocketed her pride and wrote to Disraeli (now Lord Beaconsfield) in support of the eminent statistician, Dr Farr, for the post of Registrar-General. There was no acknowledgement and another man was appointed; but the following year, thanks to strenuous lobbying from Miss Nightingale, Farr was created a Companion of the Order of the Bath by Sir Stafford Northcote.

On arrival in India Lady Lytton (who was pregnant) and two young daughters travelled directly to Simla, while the new Viceroy remained in Calcutta for the installation ceremony. He flouted tradition by making a speech; but although some eyebrows were raised, it was generally well received. Lytton then set about tackling the intricacies of Anglo-Indian administration, finding the work "puzzling and strange . . . but intensely interesting".

Meanwhile Lady Lytton, after a long journey by rail,

carriage, and finally tongas (small two-wheel covered carts drawn by two ponies), was settling her young family in Government House, Peterhof. This unpretentious building, perched on top of a little hill, was rented from the Maharaja of Simur. Members of staff were housed in nearby bungalows.

Simla was a British enclave in the foothills of the Himalayas, surrounded by native states where the wives and children of the Raj – and, more briefly, their hard-working husbands – could escape the scorching heat of the plains in summer. In the Lyttons' time there were some four hundred houses clinging to the steep slopes, which rose 7,000 to 8,000 feet above sea level. The town had one main street with two hotels, a club, a library, a bank, town hall and post office. For entertainment there were the assembly rooms for concerts, a theatre for amateur

The Viceroys' lodge, Peterhof at Simla

productions and a hall for roller-skating. Edwin Lutyens, architect of New Delhi, would later describe the site as "heroic", adding: "if one were told that monkeys had built it all, one could only say 'what wonderful monkeys – they must be shot if they do it again'."

Mary Lutyens, granddaughter of the Viceroy, had access to Edith Lytton's personal letters to her mother and twin sister, and in 1979 published a very detailed and lively account of the Lyttons' viceregal years. Edith Lytton's letters make uncomfortable reading: she was not drawn to the social life in Simla, found the English wives "either dowdy or fast", and complained about the servants. Lord Lytton's Private Secretary, Colonel Owen Burne (who had served both Mayo and Northbrook) was with the Viceroy in Calcutta; his meek wife (also expecting a child) was not a lively companion. The Burnes had their own residence in Simla, but the family went to Peterhof for meals and their two sons shared a governess with Betty and Connie Lytton. The children disliked each other and the governess was not a success, being too apt to push herself forward on social occasions.

Poor Edith Lytton. There are many good reports of her beauty and charm and her gifts as a hostess on the great occasions, but she lived by a rigid moral and social code and found it difficult to make close friends. At an uncomfortable stage of pregnancy she found the current fashion in dress "not good for ladies over twenty and certainly not for those in the family way". She adored her husband and missed him desperately in the early days;

when after two weeks in Calcutta he rejoined his family there was great rejoicing, but he was in poor health and there was much work to be done.

At the time of his appointment Disraeli had privately commanded Lytton to woo the Indian princes and subdue the unruly Afghans, but first and foremost to provide a splendid stage setting for the imminent proclamation of Queen Victoria as Empress of India. Both men shared the vision of a grand ceremony which would recall the splendours of the Moghul dynasty, while emphasizing the present might of imperial Britain as ruler and protector of the Indian people. Lytton now immersed himself in plans for a great assemblage to which all princes and maharajas who had proved loyal to the British would be invited.

Delhi, capital of the old Moghul empire, was chosen as the meeting place for the Imperial Assemblage, on a site to the north-west of the city. Tents for the use of the Lyttons, their staff, and fifty-nine guests lined a wide thoroughfare, laid with turf and flowers, leading to a vast pavilion with at one end the Viceroy's throne, eighty feet high, draped in scarlet. Lighting was provided by three-branched cast-iron lamp standards designed by Lockwood Kipling (father of Rudyard), Principal of the Mayo School of Art at Lahore. Val Prinsep RA, the official artist commissioned by the Indian Government, described the effect as outdoing the Crystal Palace in "hideosity".

The train bearing the Viceroy and his family arrived in Delhi on 23 December 1876. They mounted a very large bedecked elephant which moved at a slow pace through the narrow streets. The following day was free of engagements. On Christmas morning divine service was held in the Viceroy's camp, but Lytton could not attend. News had reached him that famine had spread to Madras. The Governor, the Duke of Buckingham, had set up poorly-run refugee camps for the survivors, which were proving very costly. Lytton held a hasty meeting with the Governors of Madras and Bombay, and Sir Richard Temple, whose knowledge of famine control stemmed from his involvement in the Bihar outbreak in 1874.

During the following four days Lytton received a constant stream of princes and maharajas. As each arrived with his splendid retinue a salute of guns was fired – the number according to rank – and the ruler was presented with an embroidered silken standard. Lady Lytton also received official guests during this period, including the young Begum of Bhopal – the only female ruler of a state – who had taken a house in Delhi for a week and had a state coach built in London for the occasion.

The day of proclamation, 1 January 1877, was declared a public holiday. The weather was perfect. Lord Lytton wore the magnificent robe of the Grand Master of the Star of India, a beautiful blue velvet embroidered with gold flowers, with an ermine cape. Lady Lytton's gown was designed (as were all her clothes) by the Parisian designer Worth. The Queen's proclamation was read in both English and Urdu. The Viceroy's speech was

Lord Lytton seated on the Viceregal throne

conventional, but elegantly phrased, ending with "God save Victoria, Queen of the United Kingdom and Empress of India". Three days of receptions, dinners and presentation of medals followed. Soon after the last guests had departed there was a tremendous thunderstorm and heavy rain which turned the campsite into a sea of red mud.

Lytton wrote an enthusiastic report to the Queen, praising the efficiency of all responsible for the arrangements and assuring Her Majesty that expenditure of public money had been "scrupulously moderate". He stressed that the princes had been loud in their expressions of praise and gratitude for the generous hospitality they had received.

But according to Prinsep, who stayed on in Delhi to complete his artistic impressions of the event, there was discontent among the members of the British community, who felt that everything had been arranged in favour of the "Black Raj". There had, for example, been no balls or other occasions when natives were not present and the ladies could dance and wear their new gowns. *The Calcutta Statesman*, although European-owned, was particularly sympathetic to the Indians and commented on 6 January: "We trust that we have now seen the last of these ceremonials for a long while to come. The atmosphere of our relations, both with the Princes and people of India, is an anachronism, with the land full of high schools, colleges and universities; and it is more than time that we abandoned this treating of the people as children. They long to be spoken to as men like ourselves, and there is a sickness in the tinsel pageantry of all these proceedings that makes us long for the simplicity of a strong, just and manly word in the country in its place."

Lytton's personal behaviour was viewed with increasing disfavour, not only by members of the Anglo-Indian community, but also in the British and Indian press. He enjoyed late-night sessions, with wine flowing and endless cigars, and lively conversation with close friends and aides. By his own admission he was a great flirt, an admirer of pretty, witty women, and on formal occasions would draw apart with a favoured companion instead of circulating among his guests. His wife, wisely, made light of these platonic flirtations, but was certainly hurt by Lytton's behaviour. She remained throughout their lives together loyal and caring. Lytton attempted to control the Indian press by passing the Vernacular Press Act: this subjected newspapers published in Indian languages to a form of censorship – an action bitterly resented by the rising class of young educated Indians who saw it as a form of racial discrimination.

The Viceroy worked long hours, liaising well with the Secretary of State, Lord Salisbury, and his own loyal staff. He found the daily inflow of telegrams, reports, statistics and committee papers an "incessant grind". As a dedicated supporter of free trade, he repealed the duties on cotton imports (against the advice of his executive council) and planned a radical reform of the customs and excise system. His efforts to improve the railway system were foiled by financial constraints.

It is, however, widely acknowledged that Lytton's enduring legacy was the control of famine in India. The failure of the April rains in 1877 had affected crops over wide areas of Bombay and Madras and the neighbouring states of Mysore and Hyderabad. In Bombay Sir Philip Wodehouse's policy of starting up large public works providing work and wages for the able-bodied, while the Government controlled the supply of food to the weak and needy, was working well. In Madras the Governor, the Duke of Buckingham, had adopted a different and potentially disastrous policy. He made huge purchases of grain at great cost and opened up relief camps for

A drawing of victims praying to the god Nandi for relief from the Famine

both the weak and able-bodied, leading to severe over-crowding. Outbreaks of disease were the inevitable outcome.

The Viceroy, together with Sir Richard Temple, Governor of Bombay, and General Michael Kennedy, Secretary of the Bombay Public Works Department, visited many of the camps, and wrote to Lady Lytton on 2 September: "You never saw such 'popular picnics' . . . The people in them do no work of any kind, are bursting with fat, and naturally enjoy themselves thoroughly . . . But the terrible question is how the Madras Government is ever to get these demoralised masses on to really useful work."

Lytton dreaded the meeting with the Duke of Buckingham – a man quick to anger and intransigence at any hint of interference. In the event the discussion went surprisingly well; Kennedy reported that the Viceroy handled the Duke "with rare tact". It was agreed that the Governor, working with General Kennedy, would control the policy that had proved so successful in Bombay, and by October 1877 Lytton was able to inform the Queen that there was a marked improvement in Madras and Mysore, largely attributable to Kennedy, who was knighted the following year. With the arrival of the autumn rains the numbers on famine relief dropped from two million to 444,000 in December 1877.

In London the Lord Mayor launched a fund for famine relief and the Duke of Buckingham's Madras Charitable Relief Committee raised funds to help the ryots to buy back the agricultural implements they had been forced to sell to feed their families. Florence Nightingale sent a donation to the Lord Mayor with a letter dated 17 August 1877, encouraging others to give: *"If English people knew what an Indian famine is – worse than a battlefield, worse even than a retreat; and this famine, too, is in its second year – there is not an English man, woman or child, who would not give out of their abundance, or out of their economy".*

Lytton received words of praise from all quarters, but

realized there was more work to be done. It was no longer possible to rely on *ad hoc* action as each famine occurred. In the Indian Government's next budget there were measures to build up a Famine Relief Fund with annual contributions amounting to £1,350,000 for the construction of irrigation works, railways and canals. And in January 1888 Lytton set up a Commission for the formulation of a Famine Code ensuring that immediate action could be taken in the case of all future outbreaks without time-wasting discussion on the course to be adopted. The Code was still in place and working well at the time of Independence in 1947.

As charged by Disraeli, Lytton had created a lavish extravaganza for the Proclamation and generously rewarded the loyal princes, stating confidently in his report to the Queen: ". . . if we have with us the princes, we shall have with us the people". But there was still the intractable Afghan problem to be resolved. Both Lawrence and Mayo had recognized the strength of Afghan resistance to interference and followed a policy of masterly inactivity, believing that the Afghans were the best defenders of their own independence. With the steady advance of Russian influence in Central Asia, Disraeli and Salisbury now advocated a forward policy, a view shared by the new Viceroy.

Soon after his arrival in Calcutta, Lytton composed a courteous missive to the wily Amir, Sher Ali, requesting that he receive a British emissary for discussions on an Anglo-Afghan treaty. The emissary was rebuffed, and a formal invitation to the Assemblage in Delhi was ignored. Lytton was furious – especially as there was news of a

Russian mission on its way to Kabul. Disraeli's cabinet urged caution, but the Viceroy felt British influence was being undermined and plunged into the Second Afghan War. A three-pronged force made its way through the mountain passes to the gates of Kabul; Sher Ali was forced to flee and died the following year. His elder son, Yakub Khan, became Amir. He feared his unruly tribesmen and welcomed British protection, readily agreeing to the establishment of a permanent residency in Kabul.

Lytton's close friend, Major Louis Cavagnari, was appointed resident and went ahead of his family to Kabul. His early reports indicated that calm had been restored in the city, but – after a brief message – "all well" – was

"Save me from my friends!" The Amir Sher Ali of Afghanistan stands trapped between the Russian Bear and the British Lion in a *Punch* cartoon of 1878

despatched on 2 September 1879, news reached the Viceroy that the residency had been stormed the following day by a fierce mob led by unpaid and mutinous soldiers. Cavagnari, his staff, and a small military escort resisted bravely. All were massacred.

Lytton, with full authority from London, despatched a strong force under the command of General Roberts which fought its way to Kabul after four weeks of fierce resistance. Alarming reports of atrocities on both sides surfaced in Britain and Gladstone condemned the war as "reckless aggression, unworthy of a Christian nation". Publication of the cost of the war caused yet more trouble for the Conservatives. From an original estimate of £5,750,000, the figure had risen to £17,490,000. (The discrepancy was later thought to be an accounting error,

Sir Louis Cavagnari seated next to Amir Yakub Khan of Afghanistan. Cavangnari would be killed by rebellious troops in Kabul several months later

but the harm had been done.) At the general election in March 1880 the Liberals swept into power and Disraeli (now Lord Beaconsfield) resigned. Lytton immediately tendered his resignation to the Queen, who responded with a sympathetic letter. He was created Earl of Lytton on Disraeli's warm recommendation. Edith, now Countess of Lytton, wrote to her mother: "We are very pleased that darling Robey should get the honours which mark his hard work having been approved . . . It will be a pauper Earldom but still in many ways perhaps it may be an advantage to the girls. I assure you I shall be very stingy . . . but dear R. has extravagant tastes, and though he may go to London as a bachelor he may yet spend a good deal".

Gladstone took swift action, appointing Lord Ripon as the new Viceroy with instructions to proceed to India without delay and withdraw all the troops from Afghanistan. Lytton's young family had been in poor health during the winter and, at the height of summer, Lytton felt he could not subject them to the three-day journey by train to Bombay. He requested the Queen's permission to delay his departure until the monsoon brought cooler weather. The Lyttons moved from Peterhof into rented accommodation in Simla. The two Viceroys met briefly and amicably, and in June 1880 the Earl of Lytton and his family departed for Bombay and boarded the troopship *Himalaya* for the voyage to England.

The return to Knebworth was a splendid and very happy occasion; the railway station at Stevenage was decked with flags and all the tenants on the estate lined

the route. For the next seven years Lytton would be free
of official duties, apart from three speeches in the House
of Lords, which were well received. It should have been
a tranquil time for the family, but he was deeply embittered by memories of the years in India and could not
find peace. He travelled alone a great deal and – ever
the incorrigible romantic – fell in love, at the age of
fifty-two with a young American actress, Mary Anderson,
who was appearing in London in his father's play *The
Lady of Lyons*. She returned his affection, but as a staunch
Catholic refused to become his mistress. Lytton made
no secret of his passion and, as always, his wife suffered
in loyal silence. An offer from Lord Salisbury of the
post of ambassador in Paris put an end to the affair.

Lytton enjoyed the French way of life and the French
admired his style and happily accepted his eccentricities.
The British Embassy became celebrated, not only for
its excellent chef, but as a brilliant literary salon. Death
came suddenly on 24 November 1891 from a cerebral
haemorrhage and, after a state funeral in Paris, the Earl
of Lytton was interred in the family mausoleum at Knebworth.

Robert Lytton defied analysis. In a letter to Mrs C W
Earle (Enid Lytton's elder sister), dated 16 February 1890,
he acknowledged his wayward personality: "I think I am
as variable as a wind, and I certainly am conscious that
I don't know myself. All I know is that I have at least
half-a-dozen persons in me, each utterly unlike the other
– all pulling different ways, and continually getting in

each other's way – and I don't think anybody else knows all of them a bit better than I do myself".

Edith Lytton lived on to the age of ninety-five, surrounded by her supportive family of two sons and three daughters. (Two children died in infancy.) She became Lady-in-Waiting to Queen Victoria and, after Victoria's death, to Queen Alexandra. Her elder son, Victor, succeeded to the earldom and served as Governor of Bengal and acting Viceroy of India. The girls all married well.

Florence Nightingale remained aloof; there is no record of correspondence with the Lyttons. The Viceroy, despite his excellent work for famine control in India, would not have measured up to the calibre of the men she had known and worked with so well during the post-Crimean years. Her biographer sums up Lytton's viceroyalty in one short sentence as ". . . more famous for the forward policy in Afghanistan than for internal reforms".

Chapter 7

George Frederick Samuel Robinson
First Marquess of Ripon (1827–1909)
Viceroy 1880–1884

"Unless we provide these men [Indian subjects] with outlets for their political aspirations they will become most naturally our bitter and very dangerous opponents . . . it is our duty to raise the people of this country politically and socially . . . making the natives the friends instead of the enemies of our rule."

Opinions on Lord Ripon, both the man and his career, differ widely from one biographer to another; some are passionate supporters, others – perhaps inevitably – detractors. There was the young George Robinson, Liberal politician, a Gladstone follower, but "without his mentor's eloquence or drive." Next the earnest seeker after truth with increasingly radical views – wildly at variance with his aristocratic background and inheritance of titles, wealth and estates. His dramatic conversion in 1873 to Roman Catholicism caused dismay in Liberal ranks and a furious reaction by anti-Catholic Englishmen.

Ripon accepted the Indian viceroyship after some misgivings because of his wife's fragile health, but approached the task with a determination to do all in his power to lead the Subcontinent to eventual self-government. In this endeavour, although supported by Gladstone, he was only partially successful. After a remarkably warm farewell from his Indian friends – and with some relief on the part of the Anglo-Indian community – he returned to England where he met indifference in Whitehall and the press, an attitude fiercely criticised by Florence Nightingale. His long retirement was marked by a softening of his radicalism and the acceptance that Indian reforms could progress only slowly because of apathy and lack of education.

George Robinson entered political life as Liberal member for Hull in 1852, but was unseated when corrupt electioneering practices (of which he was unaware) were uncovered. He was returned as member for Huddersfield in 1853 and later represented the West Riding of Yorkshire until his elevation to the Ripon title in 1871. During this period he travelled in Belgium, Italy, Switzerland and France, and became deeply involved in the Christian socialist movement. Co-operative workshops set up in the early days of the French Commune made a lasting impression on him, leading to involvement in similar experiments in England and later India.

Through the deaths of his father and uncle, Lord de

Grey (as he then became known) inherited two ancient titles, great wealth, and large estates in Lincolnshire and the West Riding, with entry to Palmerston's Liberal cabinet as Under-Secretary of State for War. Sidney Herbert was then Secretary.

Like other radical thinkers de Grey welcomed the Crimean War of 1854–6 against Russian territorial ambitions, but was worried by shortcomings in army administration and conditions in barracks, both at home and in India. His desire to improve the lot of the common soldier endeared him to Miss Nightingale and they frequently consulted on War Office matters. On Sidney Herbert's death, Florence's former suitor, R Monckton Milnes – who remained a close friend – wrote commending Lord de Grey as a genuine reformer, "willing to do all in his power to forward your great and wise designs", adding "he has considerable tact and adroitness", but "without much originality".

In 1873 Ripon experienced a midlife crisis which led to his resignation from government in August of that year. Contributing factors may have been delayed reaction to the death of his mother in 1867, a near-fatal accident to his son (the only surviving child of his marriage) in 1873, and possibly a degree of political disillusionment. He was certainly troubled about the validity of his religious faith and spent many solitary hours reading and meditating in the seclusion of his study.

Ripon's announcement of his conversion to the Roman Catholic Church in September 1874 coincided with Pope

Pius IX's publication of the Syllabus of Errors and the doctrine of papal infallibility, which had raised a storm of protest from anti-Catholics in England. *The Times* launched a savage attack on Ripon, ending with the words: "To become a Roman Catholic and remain a thorough Englishman are – it cannot be disguised – almost incompatible conditions". Gladstone appeared to share this view in a pamphlet he wrote at the time, *The Vatican Decrees in their Bearing on Civil Allegiance*, but did not entirely desert his friend. In a letter to Lord Acton in October 1874 Gladstone wrote "My belief is that no friend was in the slightest degree aware of Ripon's intentions. He is an excellent fellow . . . at least he has been: may it all continue."

For four years Ripon distanced himself from the political scene, first travelling in Italy, then spending time at his estates at Nocton and Studley Royal and resuming his studies in religion and politics. By 1880 the furore over his conversion had subsided and, in the flush of a Liberal victory, Gladstone felt sufficiently secure to put forward Ripon's name as a candidate for the post of Viceroy of India, to replace the discredited Lytton. There were rumblings, but no serious opposition. The Queen, however, queried Ripon's fitness for the viceroyalty. She did not think him sufficiently strong-willed or firm and would have preferred "someone who has more determination and energy", but would seem to have been reassured by the Prime Minister. Florence Nightingale had no such doubts. She was delighted that the Liberals were back in power and relieved by Ripon's appointment in the spring

of 1880, particularly as the two previous Viceroys, Northbrook and Lytton, had done little to forward her sanitary
campaign. But her biographer, Cook, finds it curious that
she made no private note of her feelings at this time nor
any record of a letter or visit from Ripon. Their correspondence was resumed soon after Ripon's arrival in India
in June 1880 to take up his appointment and Cook considers
that the Viceroy's stream of letters and confidential reports
on the development of his policies was one of the
"absorbing interests" which occupied Miss Nightingale
during the next four years. She wrote encouraging letters
and bombarded him with suggestions for further reforms
– for example, a scheme for village sanitation. However,
Cook suggests that during this period Miss Nightingale
"kept her feet on the ground"; she may have seen

Lord and Lady Ripon seated with their staff and dog, Ponto

Ripon as the divine instrument for vast changes in India, but she was in close touch with her "sanitarian" converts.

Sir William Wedderburn was a constant supporter, replacing the ageing Dr Sutherland, and Sir Douglas Galton kept in touch from the War Office. She made contact with A O Hume, "the father of the Indian Congress" and various Indian gentlemen, but was losing faith in the efficacy of legislative reform, believing that greater efforts were needed, both by Anglo-Indian administrators and educated Indians for the progress of the campaign for sanitation and irrigation.

Ripon's first commitment as Viceroy was reversal of the "forward" policy in Afghanistan. Abdur Rahman had been installed as Amir in Kabul. The fact that he had been a protege of the Russians was not felt to be a threat while the British dominated in the south of the country and controlled the passes to Kabul. However, almost immediately after his arrival Ripon was faced with a new crisis in the region. Ayub Khan, seeking a power base at Kandahar, defeated General Burrows in an engagement at Maiwand on 27 July 1880. The Kandahar garrison was at risk, but General Roberts marched swiftly from Kabul and restored calm, enabling Ripon to negotiate from strength a settlement by which Kabul and Kandahar were reunited and handed over to Abdul Rahman. In his biography of the Viceroy, S Gopal writes: "thereafter throughout Ripon's viceroyalty the frontier enjoyed almost unbroken tranquillity and there was much good feeling between the British and the tribes, essentially a tribute to the efficacy of a pacific approach."

The retention of Kandahar had been strongly advocated by the Queen and a majority of the Executive Council in India, but the Secretary of State, Lord Hartington, gave the Viceroy full discretion regarding the timetable for withdrawal. Ripon was convinced that a government in Kabul, set up and supported by the British, would fall as soon as that support was removed. Within a month Kandahar was handed over to a governor appointed by Abdur Rahman and, against the wishes of the Council in London, Ripon retained provisional control of Pishin and Sibi partly for strategic reasons, and partly because he felt that to do so would be a breach of faith with the tribesmen and with the Khan of Khalat.

Russia continued to pose a threat, while the breakdown of diplomatic relations with Upper Burma on India's north-east frontier had resulted in the withdrawal of the British resident. In London sabres were rattling, but Ripon refused to contemplate military action. His efforts to negotiate a treaty failed. The development of French influence in Upper Burma was a further cause for concern, but Ripon was still totally opposed to annexation, writing to the new Secretary of State, Lord Kimberley on 29 August 1884: "Our only real interest in Upper Burma is our trade, and so long as that is not seriously interfered with I should be content."

Despite the demands of the border crises, Ripon was mindful of his promise "to do some little good for India".

An engraving of General Roberts' victory over the Amir Ayub Khan and the recapture of Kabul and Kandahar

He was well acquainted with the working of the Factory Acts in England and early in his viceroyship moved to establish factory regulation in India. By 1882–3 there were sixty-two cotton mills, mainly in the Bombay Presidency, and eighteen jute mills in Bengal. Work in the mills – which employed large numbers of women and children – was exhausting and dangerous with no limitation on the hours of labour. In 1877 Lord Lytton had proposed a law prohibiting the employment of children under fourteen years of age for more than eight hours a day and for all children to be kept away from dangerous machinery. There was little support from local governments and Sir Ashley Eden, Lieutenant-Governor of Bengal, persuaded Lytton to postpone the legislation.

Ripon re-opened the discussion with a proposal for a general bill; he had the support of his executive council with only one dissenting voice, but Hartington was opposed to a uniform law across India and once again Sir Ashley Eden fought for amendments to the bill. Finally Ripon had to compromise and on 1 July 1881 the Act came into force, ensuring that no child under seven years could be employed in a factory and that children under twelve could not work for more than nine hours a day, or on dangerous work, or in two factories on the same day. Gopal sees this as one of the happier results of Ripon's administration, but the Viceroy was all too aware of its imperfections.

Repeal of Lytton's Vernacular Press Act was carried

through in 1882 in the face of opposition by both the India Council in London and his own legislative council, but with Hartington's full support on this occasion. Fifty-eight editors of vernacular journals from all parts of the Subcontinent thanked the Viceroy and assured him that "as representatives of the people and loyal subjects of the Empress, they would strive, as they had always done, to prove equal to the grave responsibilities of freedom". Gopal sums up the restoration of the liberty of the Indian press as a return to a noble tradition, resuscitating the two great doctrines of a free press and the rule of law. Some progress was made in efforts to improve elementary education and famine control. Ripon's Land Tenure Bill, an attempt to provide tenants with fixity of tenure, fair rents and free sale, was a failure, although stoutly defended by Florence Nightingale. For some years she had been involved in the development of irrigation and agriculture in India. Her article dated 30 July 1874 on *"Irrigation and Means of Transit in India"* had appeared in the *Illustrated London News* and was reprinted in the *Journal of the National Indian Association* in September 1874. Her paper in support of the Land Tenure Bill, *"The Dumb shall speak and the Deaf shall hear, or The Ryot, the Zemindar and the Government"* was read by Frederick Verney at a meeting of the East India Association in Exeter Hall on 1 June 1883 with Sir Bartle Frere in the chair. Many distinguished Anglo-Indians were present. The paper was later produced as a pamphlet and widely distributed but, like much else attempted in 1883, the Bill was heading for defeat.

Ripon's proposals for a system of self-government for both town and country proved more successful in spite of strong opposition from the Secretary of State and the India Council. By 1884 he had succeeded in establishing in all provinces a legislative framework of self-governing local authorities, despite hostility from British officials and Indian apathy. All committees, both urban and rural, had a solid preponderance of non-official members, with other members elected as necessary. Gopal sees the Act as "a laudable measure of practical idealism . . . The Government could be accused neither of inaction nor of going too fast and too far. It was a step in the right direction with many advantages and no drawbacks. And as such, it received an enthusiastic welcome from thoughtful Indian opinion." There was, however, a growing feeling in England and in the Anglo-Indian community that the Viceroy was "going too far and introducing too many changes".

The Ilbert Bill (so called after Sir C P Ilbert who introduced the Bill on 2 February 1883) was a disastrous attempt to allow Indian magistrates and district judges to exercise jurisdiction over European subjects. It provoked a furious reaction from Anglo-Indians. Under pressure from the new Secretary of State, Lord Kimberley, a compromise was reached allowing Europeans trial by jury, but the effects were far-reaching. Educated Indians had witnessed the power of well-organised rebellion; the Indian Association of Bengal held its first conference in December

1883 leading to the Congress Movement two years later – a first step towards independence.

In July 1883 Florence Nightingale was invited by Queen Victoria to Windsor to receive the decoration of the Royal Red Cross. She declined for health reasons but – somewhat daringly – took the opportunity to write to the Queen in defence of the Ilbert Bill, pointing out that the 1858 Proclamation had promised to allow the natives of India *"to share in the government of that country without distinction of race or creed"*. Sir Henry Ponsonby replied austerely on 13 August 1883 that Her Majesty "deplored the acrimony with which the question had been treated: but as it is a matter under consideration of Her Majesty's Government, the Queen is unwilling to express any opinion upon the measure at present".

Lord Ripon's policies were increasingly condemned as unrealistic and sentimental. In a letter to W E Forster in May 1883 he refuted the charge of sentimentality and referred to the rising class of educated Indians with the warning: "Unless we provide these men with outlets for their political aspirations they will become most naturally our bitter and very dangerous opponents. The consideration which has weighed most with me has been this hourly increasing importance, nay I will say necessity, of making educated natives the friends instead of the enemies of our rule." Ripon decided to take early retirement and handed over to his successor Lord Dufferin on 13 December 1884. Florence Nightingale wrote an emotional note accusing her old friend of *"deserting the Empire".* In a lengthy reply Ripon explained that he felt he had exhausted his powers of usefulness in India.

Chapter 8

Lord Dufferin (1826–1902)
Viceroy 1884–88

*". . . imaginative, sympathetic, warm-hearted and gloriously versatile
. . . his charm and gaiety tended to eclipse his more solid virtues;
but he was deliberate and unwavering in public policy."*

The Viceroys Mayo and Dufferin had much in common:
each had inherited a title and estate in the north of Ireland
and, wherever they travelled in the world, felt the strong
pull of their Irish roots. Both were caring landlords and
made strenuous efforts during the potato famine to support
the victims – but there the resemblance ends.

Lord Mayo's family was large, loving and deeply religious. He combined warmth and charm with a steadfast
character, and his viceroyalty was widely acknowledged
to be the most successful of the Imperial heyday.

By contrast, Frederick Lord Dufferin was born the only

child of a fragile 18-year-old mother. The Dufferin line of solid county squires was broken by his father, who chose a naval career and, much to the disquiet of his parents, married the granddaughter of the celebrated playwright Richard Brinsley Sheridan. The Sheridans were a brilliant and strikingly attractive clan of Irish descent who, over the course of two centuries, alternately entertained society with their gifts of oratory, wit and literary genius, and scandalised it by their erratic behaviour and reckless extravagance.

Sheridan wooed an exquisite singer, Eliza Linley, fighting two duels on her behalf, and eventually in March 1772 persuaded her to give up her stage career for a runaway marriage and love in a cottage. Joshua Reynolds painted a wistful portrait of Eliza in 1779. Their son Thomas was a consumptive and held an unremarkable post at the Cape of Good Hope until his early death. The widow returned to England with seven children and little money, but useful connections. The family was housed in an apartment at Hampton Court. Helen, one of the three beautiful daughters, married the Dufferin heir, Price Blackwood, against his parents' wishes.

Immediately after the wedding ceremony in July 1825 the young couple left for Italy, staying first in Florence, then in Siena, returning to Florence for Frederick's birth on 21 June 1826. After two years they returned to England and moved into a cottage at Long Ditton, close to Helen's mother at Hampton Court. Finally, Price Blackwood's estrangement from his family ended and they spent time at their estate, Clandeboye in County Antrim. When Price

Blackwood, now Captain Blackwood, was appointed to command the frigate HMS *Imogen*, involving long tours of duty abroad, his wife moved back to Long Ditton.

Frederick had a patchy education, first at Mr Walton's school at Hampton, known for the headmaster's energetic flogging of his pupils and for doses of brimstone and treacle. In May 1839 he was enrolled in Mr Cooksley's house at Eton, which had a reputation for less stringent discipline. On the death of his father in 1841, Frederick – then fifteen years of age – inherited the Dufferin title and the family estate. Lady Dufferin, in delicate health, was staying at Castellamare when her husband died. Frederick spent six months with her, only returning to Eton for two brief periods before leaving in April 1843.

In the interval of eighteen months before going up to Oxford, Frederick mapped out a personal programme of study and religious observance and planned improvements to his estate. The whereabouts of Helen, Lady Dufferin, at this formative stage of her son's life, are not recorded in detail, but she kept in close touch by letter. In July 1844 Dufferin wrote that he was looking forward to university life and had "a great longing for a more extensive circle of acquaintances". He was fortunate in having an uncle and guardian, Sir James Graham, who escorted him to Oxford and saw him comfortably settled in Christ Church with all the privileges of a gentleman commoner. "He was during his life at Oxford strongly dominated by religious feeling", but he showed no desire to affiliate with any particular movement or church.

It is not surprising that, given his haphazard education, there is little mention of tutors or studies, but he clearly enjoyed the varied social life and made a few close friends. His main achievement was the founding of the Pythic Club. The members met in strict privacy and took themselves very seriously, reading aloud papers on a variety of subjects. Dufferin sent his mother full reports of the proceedings, but may well have been deflated by her comments: "You are very careless in spelling . . . a habit of inattention to that matter easily grows on one . . . My grandfather Sheridan always affirmed that no Irish peer could spell. Pray don't let his first great-grandson be a proof of his knowledge of Irish ignorance." On another occasion, in reply to a letter about a frivolous entertainment Dufferin had arranged with friends, his mother wrote: "your tableaux vivants sound to me much like bad pantomimes . . . silly people putting themselves in affected attitudes to represent imaginary persons, has always appeared to me a waste of time, energy, and candlelight."

Yet she loved her son: "You are to me, my darling! All that a mother's heart can deserve, the best and most obedient of sons, but I wish you to be yet more – I wish you to be a good and great man, a philosopher and a Christian." A tall order for a young man, barely 20 years of age and bearing heavy responsibilities, but with little education and without a father to counsel him.

When Lord Dufferin was elected to the Oxford Union he made what he believed was "a pretty good speech". He took his degree in November 1846 and left Oxford the following month. In 1847 he was elected President of the Union. Later in life he wrote to Lord Arthur Russell: "Certainly my two years at Oxford were by far the happiest of my (unmarried) existence; and the friends I made there have been friends for life."

In 1847 he went with a university friend, George Boyle, to Skibbereen in County Kerry where the potato famine was ravaging the countryside. Starving people lay dying in hovels with scarcely enough strength to bury their dead, while some of the larger farmers continued to export corn and make substantial profits. Returning to Oxford Dufferin and Boyle published an account of their journey, collected donations for the famine victims, and promoted the organisation of relief committees.

Dufferin came of age in June 1847 and insisted that the celebration be held at Clandeboye. (Helen, Lady Dufferin, referred to this as "his very first act of independence".)

Five hundred tenants gathered to welcome him and hear his address, which Dufferin's uncle A B Sheridan described as "in the best taste and as graceful as a Sheridan could wish". The following year the young landlord travelled round his estate collecting details of the tenants' misfortunes over the past 20 years. He described his estate as mostly "a bleak, bare country studded thickly with the gables of ruined houses, and blotted over with low black cabins, without a hedge or a tree, but intersected with bluestone walls and flooded with black bogs, or dull steel-coloured sheets of water."

Although the conditions in Ireland weighed on his

mind, Dufferin revelled in the delights of the London season. He was, from all accounts, an attractive young man, an excellent dancer and a lively conversationalist, and he was soon caught up in a whirl of balls and dinner parties. His mother had expressed the hope that he would marry early, but should first see something of the world. She now advised him "to show no serious preferences, but to dance and chat with all impartially". Her son enjoyed flirting but tried, dutifully, to follow this sobering advice.

Dufferin was also dabbling in politics and came to the notice of the Prime Minister, Lord John Russell, who in January 1849 recommended him for the post of Lord-in-Waiting to Queen Victoria. Over a three-year period he won the favour of both the Queen and Prince Albert, although initially Her Majesty thought him "too handsome" and later commented that his Sheridan blood led him "to relax social restrictions". Dufferin was later called upon to serve as Lord of the Bedchamber from 1854 to 1858 and through his connection with the Royal Family met Viscountess Jocelyn and developed a consuming but purely chivalrous passion for the lady whom he later admitted he "never ceased to love".

In March 1895 when Queen Victoria was staying in Nice, she summoned Lord Dufferin to attend her. On his way back to Paris he stopped at Cannes to visit the cemetery and noted in his journal: "I found the tombs of poor Lady Jocelyn, Lord Roden (her eldest son) and my godson Eric Jocelyn, and left a wreath on Lady Jocelyn's. Lady Jocelyn was the earliest and dearest friend I ever had; a most beautiful, attractive, and good woman. When I knew her, she had everything that this world can give; a happy home, a husband she loved, four beautiful children – two girls and two boys; beauty, charm and popularity. She was . . . one of the Queen's ladies and one of her dearest friends."

On 31 January 1850, having advanced to the peerage, Dufferin took his seat in the House of Lords as Baron Clandboye of Clandeboye and made his maiden speech the following July, an occasion he described as a "chilling" experience. The attractions of the London season tended to conflict with his Parliamentary duties and Lady John Russell sent a kindly but firm warning that his absence from several important divisions had been noted. There were a series of political crises in 1851, but Dufferin seemed curiously uninvolved and, when Parliament rose for the autumn recess, took the opportunity to spend a winter in Rome with his mother. They stayed in a house on the Trinita di Monti and enjoyed the cosmopolitan social life of the city; Dufferin also found time to pursue his interest in art.

Dufferin's biographer, Sir Alfred Lyall, comments that his diary for the years 1852 to 1855 refers only briefly to current events at a time when there was political turmoil in England and France. Although the management of his estate "which . . . I cannot help loving better than any place in the world" and the problem of land tenures were seemingly uppermost in Dufferin's mind, he wrote a significant letter to his mother in February 1854: "Although working so hard at my poem, I still found time to concoct

a bill on Tenant Right. This I have just submitted to Sir
James Graham, and contrary to everything I dared hope,
he has assured me, that of all the bills drawn up on the
subject, mine is the best . . . Should my bill succeed in
giving satisfaction, I shall certainly feel very proud . . .
At the same time I cannot reconcile myself so easily as
you wish to the thought of discontinuing my poem. I have
never thought otherwise than you yourself with regard
to what the *main* employment of my life should be – hitherto all my studies have been chosen with the view to
fitting myself for public life . . . But in the first place,
political distinction is of very slow growth, and only the
result of a life of great drudgery and constant application, and hitherto I have not had the health to stand such
discipline, and it is very certain . . . that unless an almost
miraculous change in my constitution takes place, I can
never hope to become either a distinguished or successful
statesman. However this may be, I cannot conquer my
desire to write while I am still young, and the world indul-
gent, *not a great poem*, which I could *never* do, but one little
volume of good poetry, and this I feel as if I *could* do."

Dufferin's bill, which aimed to provide compensation
for improvements made by tenants, came before the Lords
on the last day of February 1854, but did not succeed;
the poem sank without trace.

Sir Alfred Lyall remarks further that Dufferin's diary
for the years 1852–5 "reflects singularly little of a life that
was full of opportunities" – just the usual round of social
events and development work on his estate. In 1854 he

sailed with friends to the Baltic on his yacht *Foam*. Following the outbreak of the Crimean War the British and French fleets were anchored off Aland Island preparing for an attack on a fort at Bomarsund. The young men aboard the *Foam* were invited to view the engagement from the Admiral's flagship and visited other ships directly under fire.

Dufferin revelled in the element of risk and in November 1898 wrote a lively reminiscence of the Baltic expedition for the *Cornhill Magazine*. He planned a voyage to the Crimea, but succumbed to an attack of fever and wrote a fretful letter to the Duchess of Argyll in December 1854: "My life is of an antediluvian simplicity . . . my outdoor employment is the planting of trees; the rest of the day I devote to drawing, business and brushing up on my Greek which is becoming rusty . . . I have written three or four more poems while I was in bed, but my mother, who can do so much better herself, rather discourages me".

Dufferin had his first experience of the diplomatic scene when in February 1855 he attended the Vienna Conference as an attaché to Lord John Russell. Representatives of involved European powers were meeting to agree the terms of a peace with Russia in the aftermath of the Crimean War, but in a clash of international interests caused the negotiations to drag on for seven weeks. Eventually the British envoys reached a private understanding to support a compromise proposal by Austria, but Russell was unhappy with the result and regretted his support in a speech in the House of Lords. He was bitterly attacked by his colleagues and retired from office.

Dufferin went sailing again to the Arctic and produced a book, *Letters from High Latitudes*, which was well received. In 1858 he visited Egypt, Syria, Greece and Turkey and gained some knowledge of the politics of the region, which led to Palmerston's decision to offer him the appointment of British representative on a joint European commission set up in Damascus to investigate the massacre of Christians in the Lebanon caused by blood-feuds between the Mohammedan Druses and the outnumbered Christian Maronites. Turkish rule in the Lebanon was too weak and corrupt to control the violence. The French – supported by Russia and Prussia – wanted to send in their troops. The British Government was against military action, but Dufferin was outvoted and had to agree that the French force could land at Beirut. It was a highly sensitive situation but he would seem to have held the British line with firmness, tact and charm. The French withdrew their troops and a workable solution for a period of peace in the Lebanon was agreed. In May 1861 Russell conveyed "the Queen's gracious approval of all his conduct during the whole period of his residence in Syria".

In the autumn of 1862 Dufferin married Hariot, daughter of Archibald Hamilton of Killyleagh Castle, County Down, better known as the United Irishman, Archibald Hamilton-Rowan, who was arrested and convicted of sedition in 1792, but escaped to France. The families of Blackwood and Hamilton of Killyleagh were related. Hariot was fifteen years younger than her husband, considered rather plain, but intelligent and strong-minded. It was a successful marriage; they had six sons and three daughters, and Hariot brought into Dufferin's life a much-needed order and stability. Realizing that her husband was destined for high office, she set about fitting herself for the role of consort and succeeded admirably.

Helen, Lady Dufferin, died in June 1867 after a long and painful illness. In a memoir prefixing her published *Songs and Verses* her son paid glowing tribute: "one of the sweetest, most beautiful, most accomplished, most loving and lovable human beings that ever walked this earth". In more rational mood he wrote to the Duchess of Argyll some four months later: "we are all pretty well here, my wife and children especially so. It was terrible coming back again, but the hurry and pressure of so much business was a good thing, though God knows I missed her advice and sympathy more than ever."

A year before his marriage Dufferin had commissioned Helen's Tower, a strange ungainly structure standing on a hill in sight of his home at Clandboye, and he dedicated it to his mother. He then suggested that the major poets in England might care to contribute *"epigraphical verses"*. Only Tennyson's laboured poem seems to have survived. (The poet's wife preferred an earlier and longer version.)

> Helen's Tower, here I stand,
> Dominant over sea and land.

Son's love built me, and I hold
Mother's love in lettered gold.
Would my granite girth were strong
As either love, to last as long.
I should wear my crown entire
To and thro' the Doomsday fire,
And be found of angel eyes
In earth's recurring Paradise.

Dufferin was delighted: "What I like so . . . is the quaint
Teutonic feeling which somehow seems to me to pervade
the lines . . . and that is just what I had desired."

In February 1872, following news of the assassination
of Lord Mayo, Dufferin was asked if he would allow his
name to go forward, with others, for the Viceroyalty of
India; he agreed, but Lord Northbrook was appointed.
One month later Dufferin was offered the Governorship
of Canada and accepted with alacrity. His personal
finances were in a perilous state. By the early 1870s his
debts amounted to £299,000 and he had been forced to
sell his estates in County Down, retaining only the land
circling the house at Clandboye and property at Helen's
Bay. His income from the Canadian post would relieve
the pressure.

The Dufferins set sail for Quebec in June 1872 and
the installation ceremony took place later that month.
The Governor-General had jurisdiction over a vast territory stretching from the Atlantic to the Pacific Ocean.
His priorities were to consolidate the new dominion and

strengthen its ties with Britain, but there were outstanding problems. The indigenous Indians were only partially settled in the west of the country; the vital rail link to the Pacific had still to be surveyed; there was friction between the French and English-speaking communities; and the United States was proving a difficult neighbour. The Dufferins entertained lavishly and travelled throughout Canada. There were brief visits to Detroit and Chicago to promote good-neighbourly relations. Dufferin was an effective orator and his speech at the opening of the Canadian Parliament was delivered in fluent French as well as English.

On the debit side the Governor-General dreaded the long, icy winters which he found boring and debilitating, and was relieved when his term of office ended in October 1878. Lady Dufferin had proved a popular consort and the couple left Canada on a high note following a farewell ball in Ottawa and a valedictory address from both Houses of Parliament. Mr Gladstone sent a warm message of congratulation.

Diplomatic posts at St Petersburg and Constantinople followed in quick succession. Dufferin had limited experience as a professional diplomat, but was charming, quick-witted and equally at ease with the Tsar of Russia or the Sultan of Turkey. He met the demands of both postings with reasonable success.

In 1884 Dufferin was nominated Viceroy of India on the retirement of Lord Ripon – a post he had long coveted. Lord Derby wrote of his appointment: "Dufferin is popular everywhere, having pleasant manners, ready

Lord and Lady Dufferin, 1883

wit, considerable power as a speaker and a fair share of Irish blarney". The new Viceroy called on Miss Nightingale on 5 November 1884. The following day she wrote to her sanitary expert, Dr Sutherland: *"My visit from Lord Dufferin took place yesterday. We went over many things – sanitation, land tenure, agriculture, civil service, etc etc. And I am to send him a note of each. But about sanitary things he says he is perfectly ignorant, especially of Indian sanitary things. But he says 'give me your instructions and I will obey them. I will study them on my way out. Send me what you think and I will fire the shot.'"*

This letter reached Dr Sutherland on a Friday with the request that he send his notes before *"Monday"*. The normally obedient Doctor was working on the cholera bacillus with the aid of a beautiful microscope from Vienna; this he replied, would occupy him on Friday and Saturday and Sunday, so "the Viceroy must wait". Miss Nightingale's wrath was formidable; she sent notes and telegrams: *"I did not know that the bacillus was of more consequence than a Viceroy . . . If you did a little on Sunday, the Recording Angel would drop not a tear but a smile."* Eventually calm was restored and, the two old friends set about (in Cook's words) *"indoctrinating their fifth Viceroy in the truths of their sanitary gospel".*

Dufferin acknowledged the material on 13 November in an elegant note from *SS Tasmania*: "I duly received the papers you were good enough to send me and you

The Viceregal Lodge on Observatory Hill in Simla

may be quite sure of my studying them with the attention they deserve. I know how well entitled you are to speak with authority in reference to Indian questions, and I can well believe that you may have thought out many conclusions which it would be of the greatest benefit to ponder over."

Dufferin cruised through his viceroyalty with apparent ease. He revelled in the grand ceremonial occasions and wore his splendid robes of office with panache. To the joy of the Anglo-Indian community the viceregal couple restored the glitter and gaiety to Government House so sadly lacking in the Ripon era. The Secretary of State – Randolph Churchill – was persuaded by Dufferin to fund his architectural dream of an "enchanted castle" at Simla, replacing the ramshackle Peterhof. Lord Gross, who succeeded Randolph Churchill, was probably less enchanted when faced with a bill for £100,000 for the new residence.

"In the tremendous hall, which rose through the full height of the house, everything was of teak, walnut or deodar, elaborately carved or moulded. The big drawing room was furnished with gold and brown silks; the ball-room decorated in a brighter shade of yellow; the state dining room hung with leather in rich dark colours. A white-tiled basement kitchen and electric lights were great novelties . . ."

There was a further problem in Upper Burma where France was intriguing with the young ruler, King Tibaw. The King refused in offensive terms to receive a British

A view of the Ballroom at the Viceregal Lodge, Simla

resident at Mandalay. After a brief and decisive campaign the British, with the loss of only twenty men, took over the whole country. Annexation followed with the full support of the British government – a logical step as Lower Burma was already part of the British Empire. Dufferin saw this as the climax of his viceroyalty and when in 1888 he was advanced in the Peerage he chose to become Marquess of Dufferin and Ava – Ava being the name of the ancient capital of Burma.

Dufferin recognised the growing power of the Indian middle class, still a tiny minority, but possessing for the first time "a language, ideas and attitudes in common". He supported the early work of Hume and the formation

of the Indian National Congress. But the relentless flow
of official papers appalled the Viceroy. During the
various stages of his career he had mastered the art of
delegation and now dealt with the mountain of paperwork by passing it on to his colleagues and hardworking
secretary. He avoided, as far as possible, putting pen to
paper, but essential letters to the Secretary of State were
succinct, informative and witty. In a letter dated 1
January 1888 to Sir William Gregory he wrote: "It is
an odd thing to say, but dullness is certainly the char-
acteristic of a viceroy's existence. All the people who
surround him are younger than himself, even the pretty
women who condescend to cheer him, it is better to
keep at a distance; and except occasionally, the business he has to deal with is of a very uninteresting and
terre á terre description". The fault lines in his character,
which led in his youth to long periods of boredom,
lethargy and lack of purpose were now clearly visible
in his growing disenchantment with India. He was
quietly planning early retirement at the end of 1888,
with an eye on the post of Ambassador at Rome, which
offered a more agreeable lifestyle. (In the event it was
Lady Dufferin who left a lasting impact on the Indian
people. At Queen Victoria's request she launched the
"National Association for Supplying Medical Aid to the
Women of India", subsequently known as the "Countess
of Dufferin Fund", and presided over countless meetings to raise funds for hospitals and dispensaries. By the
time she left India her initiative had been followed in

every province and in all the principal states.

In the years following her meeting with Lord Dufferin Miss Nightingale had not been idle. In 1885 – her jubilee year – she had added Sir Neville Chamberlain and Sir Peter Lumsden to her list of Anglo-Indian contacts. Lord Reay called on her in March the same year before leaving to take up the governorship of Bombay and they corresponded regularly on sanitary matters. In October Lord Roberts saw her before going out to India as Commander-in-Chief of the Army. Their discussion on reforms for the health and care of the troops bore fruit during his command. She was delighted to receive Lord Roberts' report dated 6 August 1888 that the Government had finally sanctioned the employment of nurses in the military hospitals, starting at the two large centres of Umballa and Rawalpindi. Each hospital would have eighteen nurses under the control of a lady superintendent.

Surgeon-General Arthur Payne, who was in charge of the selection process, had several meetings with Miss Nightingale, thus implementing, after twenty-two years, a scheme she had first discussed with Lord Lawrence during his viceroyalty.

A further cause for satisfaction was the relationship she developed with Lady Dufferin. She had long been interested in improved medical treatment for the women of India and Lady Dufferin consulted her at every stage of her campaign. They collaborated on producing sanitary tracts – small moral story books promoting health.

Hariot Dufferin became one of the most successful and beloved Vicereines

Miss Nightingale collected suitable material for the project.

In 1886 she received private information that the Indian sanitary service was in danger because of the need for retrenchment following the annexation of Upper Burma; the posts of the sanitary commissioners were at risk. She wrote a long letter on 5 November 1886 to Lord Dufferin who did not fail her. He referred the letter to the head of the Finance Committee, but warned Miss Nightingale not to expect an early decision. On 20 August 1887 Dufferin was able to report that the proposals for the abolition of the sanitary commissioners had been quashed, but local governments would be required to put the whole subject of sanitation on a sounder footing. In February 1888 Dufferin gave notice of retirement in the following December. He was duly appointed British Ambassador at Rome with effect from December 1888. From letters written at the time it seems that the Viceroy left India with no regrets. Lady Dufferin, who had been awarded the Star of India for her work, had the satisfaction of knowing that her guidelines had been adopted in every province and in all the principal states. Her work was commemorated at the time in a poem *Song of the Women*, by Rudyard Kipling.

How shall she know the worship that we do her?
The walls are high and she is very far.
How shall the women's message reach unto her
Above the tumult of the packed bazaar?

Free wind of March against the lattice blowing,
Bear thou our thanks lest she depart unknowing.

After a pleasant and uneventful two years in Rome, Dufferin was appointed Ambassador at Paris, succeeding Lord Lytton. He was faced with a difficult problem concerning what he described as "the tyrannical injustice' of French policy in Siam", but succeeded in calming Anglo-French colonial rivalries elsewhere. He was, perhaps, best known for his urbane and lavish hospitality at the British Embassy.

Retirement in 1896 was marred by serious financial problems. In 1900 the Dufferins received news from South Africa of the death in action of their eldest son. Lord Dufferin, now afflicted with deteriorating eyesight, became increasingly dependent on his "Little Lal" as he affectionately referred to his wife. He died on February 1902 and was buried in the private graveyard at Clandboye. Hariot, Lady Dufferin, died in 1936 aged 93.

Chapter 9

Henry Charles Keith Petty-Fitzmaurice
Fifth Marquess of Lansdowne (1845–1927)
Viceroy 1888–94

*". . . qualities of tact and reliability served him well . . . unlike
Lytton before or Curzon after, Lansdowne managed an active defence
of imperial interests without arousing controversy at home though
an avowed 'forward' policy or divisions within his government."*

Surveying the stately procession of nineteenth-century
viceroys it becomes clear that Lord Lansdowne was the
grandest of them all. The Fitzmaurices were of Norman
descent and Lords of Kerry from the thirteenth-century.
Henry, born on 14 January 1845, was the elder son of
the fourth Marquess of Lansdowne and his second wife,
Emily Jane Mercer de Flahault, Lady Nairne (a Scottish
heiress through her mother). He was known as Viscount

Frank Dicksee. 1913

Lansdowne

Clanmaurice until the death of his grandfather (the third Marquess) in 1863, and then as the Earl of Kerry until the sudden death of his father in 1866, when he inherited one of the foremost Whig titles and great estates in England, Scotland and Ireland. The principal family seats were the palatial Bowood in Wiltshire and Lansdowne House in Berkeley Square, one of the finest mansions in London. But the family's rent-roll was drastically reduced by the unrest of the 1880s and the young Marquess also inherited a massive debt.

From the age of ten Clanmaurice was educated at Mr Mind's private school at Woodcote near Reading; then at Eton where, in his mid-teens, he fell in with the boating set which "treated work lightly, with pleasure their main objective". His housemaster, Mr Birch, recommended his severance from these jolly friends. His father accepted this advice and sent his son to a private tutor, the Reverend Lewis Campbell, with instructions to prepare him for entry to Balliol College, Oxford rather than Christ Church, the usual choice for gentleman commoners.

Entry to Balliol in 1864 brought Clanmaurice under the benign influence of Dr Benjamin Jowett, shortly to become Master of the College. The death of his father led to his inheritance of the title and historic possessions, but "Clan" – as he was known – continued his studies and enjoyed a typical undergraduate's life. Jowett wrote to him in 1867 "When I pass your splendid house in London I feel a sort of wonder that the owner should be quietly reading in Oxford. But you could not do a wiser or better thing. Wealth and rank are means and not ends, and it may be the greatest evil or the greatest good as they are used". In spite of serious application to his studies the young Lord Lansdowne only achieved a second in Greats; he was deeply disappointed. Jowett responded with a bracing mixture of sympathy and sound advice. "You have certainly far greater ability than many First Classmen and by good management, with your opportunities, you may make every year a progress on the one before".

In the autumn of 1869 Lansdowne married Lady Maud Hamilton, youngest daughter of the Duke of Abercorn. It was from all accounts an ideal marriage; Lady Lansdowne possessed dignity and charm, the perfect consort for a man clearly destined for high office.

As a Whig peer Lansdowne took his seat on the Liberal benches in the House of Lords. He served as a junior minister in two Liberal administrations, but finally felt constrained to leave the party in 1880 because he could not support Gladstone's Irish Compensation for Disturbance Bill, which would lead to the sweeping Irish Land Act the following year. This defence of the landowning class from one of the largest Anglo-Irish landlords made him a prime target of the anti-landlord movement throughout his life.

In 1883 Lansdowne accepted a generous offer from Gladstone to go to Canada as Governor-General, but with some reluctance. He regretted leaving his widowed mother and the homes he loved, but needed the income. Some of his valuable pictures had been sold and he feared he

Benjamin Jowett, centre,
Master of Balliol College,
Oxford

might never be able to afford to live in Lansdowne House. Lord and Lady Lansdowne and their four children arrived in Quebec on 23 October 1883 and were welcomed by the outgoing Governor-General, Lord Lorne. Lansdowne was duly sworn in and wrote to his mother (Emily, Marchioness of Lansdowne) about the rest of the proceedings on their first day in Canada: "We drove off, still with our escort, to the Theatre, where the civic address of welcome was delivered by the Mayor, a cheery little Frenchman, M. Langelier. This he read first in French and then in English, making a bold attempt to grapple with my numerous English and French titles . . . I made a short reply, first in English and then in French; the audience – almost all French Canadians – listened respectfully to the first and cheered some of the passages, but before I had got out half a dozen words of the French reply, the whole audience burst into rapturous applause". The family then travelled by train to Ottawa and settled into the official residence, which Lansdowne found comfortable, but with "hideous furniture".

Apart from the long-running dispute with the United States over the delimitation of the Newfoundland fisheries, the political situation remained calm. Lansdowne maintained good relations with the Canadian Premier, Sir John Alexander Macdonald, throughout his period of office. There was much travelling and an endless round of social functions. Writing to his mother on 18 January 1884 Lansdowne looked forward to one reception with wry humour: "Tomorrow we have a Drawing Room, an awful occasion, but thank heavens there is no kissing. I say that without disrespect to some of the fair Canadians".

During 1887 there were no events of political importance; the Canadians' enthusiastic celebration of the Queen's Golden Jubilee underlined their lack of desire for separation and Lansdowne's popularity steadily increased. His standing in both the Liberal and Tory parties at home remained high, but a letter from Lord Salisbury dated 31 December 1887 offering the viceroyship of India took him by surprise. After time for reflection, Lansdowne reported to his mother "I have . . . been obliged to look the position in the face. I am offered a magnificent post, the most responsible and honourable outside England. It is placed within my reach while I am comparatively young, at a moment when, if ever, I ought to have some work in me".

Miss Nightingale saw Lord Lansdowne twice before he left for India. She had been scrutinising the Bombay Sanitation Bill – a measure first projected in 1887 – and sent her views to Lord Cross at the India Office and to Lord Reay in India, keeping Lord Lansdowne fully informed. Her main cause for concern was the exclusion of smaller villages from the provisions of the Bill. She wrote letters to native associations explaining the need for village sanitation and implored the National Association in Bombay to send representatives to the International Congress of Hygiene and Demography in London, chaired by her good friend Sir Douglas Galton and opened on 10 August 1891 by the Prince of Wales.

Miss Nightingale used the Indian Section of the Congress to promote her scheme to finance sanitation works from existing local taxes, but met resistance from the Indian government. Nothing daunted, she sent a memorandum embodying her proposals and signed by influential supporters to the Secretary of State, who endorsed it and forwarded the paper at once to the Indian government. A copy went to the Viceroy for circulation to local governments. Altogether, a telling example of Florence Nightingale's ability to orchestrate an effective publicity campaign. However, members of the Indian government, though sympathetic to her main objective, continued to oppose the idea of financing the work from existing taxation. Sir William Wedderburn wrote diplomatically on 7 July 1893: "You have most effectively drawn attention to the subject". And there the matter rested. At 73 years of age Miss Nightingale continued to press various Indian gentlemen with whom she corresponded to *"bestir themselves"* and launched a new plan for *"Health Missionaries for India"*.

Benjamin Jowett was deeply interested in many of Florence Nightingale's later Indian projects, especially those related to education. (He had begged her not to get involved with the intricacies of land tenure.) Jowett had been in correspondence with her for some time about the Oxford courses for Indian students, writing on 14 October 1887. "I want to prove to you that your words do sometimes affect my flighty or stony heart and are not altogether cast to the winds. Therefore I send you the last report of the Indian Students, in which you will perceive that agricultural chemistry has become a reality; and that owing to YOU (though I fear that, like so many other of your good deeds, this will never be known to men), Indian students are reading about agriculture, and that therefore Indian Ryots may have a better chance of being somewhat better fed than hitherto."

With his former student at Balliol settled in India, Jowett felt he could, "without impertinence", write suggesting how Lansdowne might become "a really great Viceroy". Would Miss Nightingale consider what this might involve? According to Cook "she took the hint most seriously: the education of Viceroys was a favourite occupation with her". She discussed possible reforms with various advisers (without revealing the purpose), then passed the edited information to Jowett, who filtered it through to Lansdowne.

The Lansdownes arrived at Bombay on 3 December 1888. Their landing was not auspicious; the steam launch transporting them to the dock "snorted" and blew coal dust over Lady Lansdowne's white frock. Later, exhausted by the reception, the heat and the journey to their temporary residence at Malabar Point, the "Lady Sahib" lay on the sofa in a minimum of clothing and was fanned by "a black female with a ring through her nose" who told her that she was much too thin. Her husband was amused by the scene. After a full social week in Bombay the Lansdowne family travelled by train to Calcutta and were welcomed by Lord Dufferin and installed in Government House. A pleasant dinner for eighty male guests had been arranged and the following day (Sunday), after attending morning service at the Cathedral, Lansdowne spent some hours in discussion with the outgoing Viceroy. The handover ceremony took place on 10 December 1888 and the new Viceroy and Vicereine drove to the station with the Dufferins. It was a somewhat mournful departure, Lord Lansdowne commenting "she (Lady Dufferin) was very low, poor woman".

At this key point in his career Lansdowne is described as slim, of medium stature, with neat side whiskers and moustache, his bearing impressive, but lightened by the courtly manners of a French *grand seigneur*. He made an excellent impression on the Anglo-Indian community and on the Princes and educated Indians, but the members of the National Congress remained restless and resentful.

Before leaving office Dufferin had given a forthright speech attacking the native demand for self-government. The reformers hoped for a changes of attitude from Lansdowne, but he refused to be drawn on potentially contentious matters at this early stage. He had, increasingly, to contend with unwelcome interference from some members of the House of Commons, who were in contact with the Congress Party of India.

In April 1889 the viceregal party moved to the cooler air of Simla. They travelled in a procession of small landaus drawn by ponies which were changed every four miles, covering a distance of some sixty miles in eight hours. The site of the new Government House was spectacular, with views of soaring mountain peaks on every side. However, Lansdowne – whose fastidious taste had been nurtured by the restrained splendours of Bowood and Lansdowne House – was not impressed by the "amateur architecture" and interior waste of space, as described in a letter to his mother dated 11 April 1889. He reserved his fiercest criticism for the carpets ". . . mostly hideous and why have they got them from Maple's when such lovely ones are made here?" Lansdowne arrived in India at a time when conditions were generally peaceful, but yet again there was trouble brewing in Afghanistan. Relations with the Amir Abdur Rahman were far from easy. Construction of a small but vital railway at Chamar was held up by the Amir's excessive demand for compensation and there were horrifying reports of cruelty and oppression under his regime. The army Commander-in-Chief, Sir Frederick Roberts, proposed a military mission to Afghanistan, but the Liberal government under Gladstone opposed any possibility of a return to a "forward" policy. Lansdowne achieved a compromise solution with the Amir, but could not resist sending a severe remonstrance to the bloodthirsty ruler.

It took Lansdowne nearly four years to achieve the Indian Council reforms which Dufferin had promised, believing they would enable moderate reformers in the Congress to rid themselves of extremists. Lord Salisbury wrote on 27 June 1890: "A bill like the Indian Councils Bill, which has some enemies and no ardent supporters, has little chance of forcing its way through." Lansdowne had been seen by the Indians as a second Ripon, but he became increasingly alienated by the erratic behaviour of Hume, the leader of the Congress, and returned to the traditional policy of strengthening the landowners against the rising educated middle class.

Towards the end of his viceroyship Lansdowne was denounced by sections of the Indian press as an "enemy of the people" and a puppet in the hands of the Civil Service. In 1882 his attempt to pass the Bengal Juries Bill – a measure introduced because of the refusal of juries in certain districts of Bengal to convict in cases of murder – produced an unexpected outcry in the Indian press and the English liberal press followed suit. The British Government became alarmed and Lansdowne contemplated resignation, but was saved by an announcement of a commission of enquiry by the new Secretary of State, Lord Kimberley.

Throughout the remainder of Lansdowne's viceroyalty, with Kimberley's support, the wheels of government ran smoothly and he continued to do everything expected of an Indian viceroy, however disagreeable to a man of his sensitive nature. He visited hospitals and a ship crammed with devout and suffering Muslims; inspected a leper colony and a veterinary hospital, but without any deep sense of mission or strong feeling for the extraordinary country he ruled. He found the climate very trying and suffered various ailments. The workload was handled efficiently, but the social life and trappings of office held no appeal, and he particularly disliked the ceremonials where Indian princes draped him in garlands and smeared him with "that horrible attar of roses".

Lansdowne's term of office ended in 1894 with the appointment of a reluctant Lord Elgin (Ninth Earl), and a year later he joined Lord Salisbury's cabinet as a Liberal Unionist. He was appointed Foreign Secretary in 1900 and continued to serve at the forefront of British politics until the First World War.

Lord Lansdowne corresponded with Florence Nightingale on sanitary matters throughout his viceroyalty and there was significant progress on public works. She commented in a private note *"He did much for us in every way"* and greatly appreciated Lansdowne's letter of 11 October 1892, written from Simla on the death of Jowett, who had been such a devoted friend to them both: "Our dear old friend is, as far as his bodily presence in our midst is concerned, lost to us. It is a real sorrow to me. I had no more constant friend, and I cannot express the gratitude with which I look back to his unfailing interest in all that befell me and to his help and guidance at times when they were most needed."

Lord Lansdowne died of heart failure aged 82 at Anmer House, Clonmel on 3 June 1927 and was buried at Bowood in Wiltshire.

Chapter 10

The Ninth Earl of Elgin
(1849–1917)
Viceroy 1894–99

"Not called on to make a political advance, and preoccupied by a series of difficult administrative problems . . . his historical reputation has also suffered from his being succeeded by the flamboyant Lord Curzon."

Victor Alexander Bruce, eldest son of the Eighth Earl and his second wife, Lady Louis Lambton, was born in Canada during his father's governorship. Victor and his three brothers attended Trinity College, Glenalmond, a Spartan Scottish school. At the age of twelve Victor moved to Eton, shortly before his father's death in the Himalayas. His widowed mother subsequently became morbidly obsessed by the memory of her late husband. Queen Victoria – still in mourning for Prince Albert –

sent Lady Elgin a gold and onyx bracelet with the inscription "From VRI, a broken-hearted widow like yourself".

After Eton, Victor went to Balliol College, Oxford, graduating in 1873 with a second class degree in literae humaniores. He came of age in 1870 with festivities at the family estate, Broomhall in Fife, and was urged to live up to the glories of his name with a song especially composed for the occasion:

> Twas with sword, spear and shield.
> He made proud Edward's force to yield
> And vanquish'd England on the field
> The field of Bannockburn . . .
> Adorn, like sires, his country's page
> And hand unstained to latest age
> The illustrious name of Bruce

For the next twenty years Elgin ran the estate and played and active part in country affairs and Scottish Liberal politics. He inherited his father's seat in the House of Lords and became a staunch supporter of the Liberal party, sharing Gladstone's mistrust of foreign imperial ventures.

Elgin was not a romantic figure; he inherited his father's short stature and snub nose, but had a fine head and cultivated a large beard. In 1876 he was married to Lady Constance Carnegie, daughter of James Carnegie, Sixth Earl of Southesk. They had eleven children: six boys and five girls.

The Earl was a loyal, conscientious man, and an effective public speaker, but aware of his inadequacies. The Foreign Secretary, Lord Rosebery, reported that he had had to walk with him for more than an hour round Arthur's Seat in Edinburgh before Elgin finally agreed to accept the viceroyalty. Compared with Lansdowne – "the Great Ornamental" – he lacked charisma, but brought to India a refreshing breath of the Scottish way of life, often seen walking briskly in comfortable country clothes with his two dogs. The trappings of viceroyalty did not appeal, although he handled the important occasions with dignity.

As an administrator Elgin was hardworking and liked by his staff. He was content to leave the major decisions to the India Office in London and the day-to-day running of the Indian government in the hands of the Council, seeing himself as a bridge between the two. He had some sympathy with the aims of the Indian Congress Party, but felt that the Indians were not yet ready for self-rule.

On succeeding Lord Lansdowne as Viceroy in January 1894, Elgin sent his private secretary, Henry Babington Smith, to call on Miss Nightingale; he became her means of communication with the Viceroy, but her days of vigorous campaigning were over. She realized that the progress of sanitation in India would inevitably be slow and accepted that there were limitations to what she could contribute. In 1896 she wrote: *"I am painfully aware how difficult, how almost impossible it is for anyone a great distance to do anything to help forward a movement requiring unremitting labour and supervision on the spot"*. In more optimistic mood she acknowledged: *"But it is my privilege to meet in England Indian friends who are heartily desirous of obtaining for their poorer fellow-countrymen the benefits which, through sanitary science, are gradually being extended to the masses, both in town and country . . ."* and went on to describe the steps which her friend Mr Malabari was taking to provide sanitary education and even to institute Health Missionaries in selected districts of rural India.

In 1898 Miss Nightingale received a visit from the Aga Khan and wrote a note of the interview: *"A most interesting man, but you could never teach him sanitation. I never understood before how difficult, how really impossible it is for an Eastern to care for material things".* She continued to lead a busy life and deal with correspondence with the help of a lady typewriter, writing to her cousin Henry Bonham Carter in September 1895: *"I have my hands full and am not idle, though people naturally think I have gone to sleep or am dead".* On 11 Februay 1897 Babington Smith wrote a letter to J P Hewett, Secretary to the Government, Home Department, enclosing a copy of a letter from Florence Nightingale referring to the scheme of Village Sanitary Inspection. She had asked for information which would not be available until publication of the Annual Reports, but Babington Smith suggested: "perhaps it may be possible to give an answer now to some of the questions, and in some cases note might be made of Miss Nightingale's suggestions, for consideration when the list of points to be dealt with comes under revision."

Another example of Florence Nightingale's persistent quest for information and Babington Smith's willing support in the name of the Viceroy comes in a letter about the proposed resiting of the Calcutta General Hospital. Vicereines had traditionally taken a close interest in this charitable institution and both Lady Dufferin and Lady Elgin would almost certainly have sought Miss Nightingale's views on nursing matters. A letter to Babington Smith dated 8 November 1897 from the Honourable H H Risley, Secretary to the Government of Bengal, reveals the depth of her involvement: "I returned from leave about the middle of last month, and found your letter of 20 September, with Miss Nightingale's suggestions about the General Hospital, waiting for me. So far I have been unable to do anything, as the officer in charge of the plans is away on short leave; but as soon as he comes back, the suggestions as to the internal arrangements of the proposed building will be carefully considered . . . Miss Nightingale also asks for information about the nursing arrangements. These have an ancient and complicated history, and I should have to write at great length to make matters clear . . . And the report of the Committee appointed by the Resolution ought to bring out the defects of the system and show what ought to improve it. I hear, however, that the proceedings of the Committee were highly controversial, and I fancy the report, when we get it, will not be an easy document to deal with!" Here was a defensive letter from a very harried civil servant.

The early days of Elgin's viceroyalty were peaceful; for once there were no problems with the Afghans, and the Russians and French were lying low. He established a

The Elgins photographed at Simla with their staff

cautious relationship with the Indian National Congress and had some sympathy with the objectives of educated Indians wishing to gain entry into government, both at central and local levels, but remained convinced that if the British wished to stay in India they must retain control of some of the senior posts in the army and civil service.

Two troublesome issues confronted the new Viceroy. There was the perennial question as to whether India should impose a tariff on imported cotton goods from Britain in order to safeguard local manufacturers. Elgin's instinct was to uphold the interests of India, but the lobbyists for the Manchester cotton trade prevailed and Elgin, against his better judgement, had to agree that the imposition of a tariff was impossible. He was widely criticized for his inept handling of the matter, both in India and Britain.

There was also the issue of the rupee which, in common with other eastern currencies, was traditionally based on silver; but in the early 1880s the world price of silver relative to gold was highly unstable. In this instance Elgin's policy that India must move to the Gold Standard was clear and consistent and by 1899 the Indian government had successfully stabilised the gold value of the rupee.

Early plans were drawn up for a programme of viceregal autumn tours through the country, involving long journeys and ceremonial set-pieces. On the first of these in 1884 a particularly splendid Durbar was held at Kermal and

Lady Elgin in a silver *tanjan*

the journey ended somberly at the grave of the Eighth Earl at Dharmsala.

Lady Elgin suffered from poor health and was easily fatigued, but enjoyed the cooler months at Simla. The family rented a simple house at Mashobra, a few miles from the centre, which they christened "The Retreat" and spent time there whenever possible. The three daughters revelled in the various festivities over the summer and Bessie, aged eighteen, was increasingly called upon to deputize for her mother on formal occasions. She kept a diary describing local events and their happy family life; one of her duties was to darn the long woollen socks her father wore on his country walks.

In 1896 there was a terrible famine due to the failure of the monsoon. The victims numbered three quarters of a million and outbreaks of plague followed. It was a testing time for Elgin. He followed the Famine Code laid down by Lord Lytton and used the new railway system to transport supplies swiftly to the stricken areas. There was praise in both England and India for his calm handling of the crisis. The plague, which was centred on the Bombay Presidency, was more difficult to deal with. The Plague Rules drawn up in accordance with Western health requirements, offended the religious beliefs of the Hindus, and the government would seem to have conducted the enforcement measures with a lack of tact. The Viceroy was criticized for his apparent inability to give firm guidance.

Disturbances on the North-West Frontier necessitated costly and difficult military campaigns, notably the Chitral disturbances in March 1895 in the disputed Kashmir territory. The British Government wished to abandon Chitral, but Elgin believed it was of strategic importance and to abandon it would be a sign of weakness. In the event the Rosebery administration fell the following June and the new Conservative government supported the Viceroy. As a result Chitral remained under British rule and that section of the frontier remained reasonably stable up to the granting of independence in 1947.

Bessie's marriage in 1898 to the indispensable Henry Babington Smith was the occasion for great rejoicing. After the service in Christ Church, Simla, a colourful procession wound its way up the hill to Viceregal Lodge in a variety of carriages and rickshaws, escorted by the Viceregal bodyguard and the Punjab Light Horse. The chef at the lodge, Tancredi, produced a six-foot-high wedding cake.

Elgin's term of office ended in 1899. In her diary Bessie described the evening the telegram arrived from London naming his successor. Her father pronounced the name "Curzon" in a low voice to his wife and daughters and, after a pause for reflection, added "Where will it go if Mr Curzon is imperious?".

The period of the Raj from 1858 to the end of the century, which Percival Spear so aptly called "The Imperial Heyday" was drawing to a close. Florence Nightingale – slowly losing sight and strength – was nearing the end of her active life. She continued to receive papers from the India Office until 1906, demonstrating the depth of her involvement with the people of India.

Chapter 11

Redressing the Balance

Histories of India written in the last sixty years tend to underrate the achievements of the nineteenth-century viceroys whose statues once lined the avenue leading to Government House in Calcutta and now rest neglected at Barrackpore, furthermore Florence Nightingale's efforts to improve the health of the Indian rural poor during the final twenty years of her active life are dismissed in a few paragraphs, or totally overlooked.

Historians have been kinder to those lesser mortals, the British civil servants – labelled "The Guardians" by Philip Woodruff in his book of the same title published in 1954. After passing the Indian Civil Service examinations at Oxford University these gifted young men set out for India imbued with the heady ideals of Benjamin Jowett and Plato's *Republic*, but soon discovered that the reality of life in the Subcontinent left little time for idealism.

A junior administrator with a district to control would spend long hours in the saddle patrolling the villages. Evenings were devoted to paperwork by the light of an oil lamp, with only a native servant or two, and perhaps a dog for company. If he could persuade a young British bride to share his life, she faced the trauma of childbirth without adequate medical attention, followed by separation from the children at an early age.

The descendants of these dedicated men and women – and there must be thousands living in Britain today – can only feel sadness, even anger, at this cavalier treatment of the age of the Raj. Surely the time is ripe for reappraisal of the massive British contribution to the infrastructure of the Subcontinent in the nineteenth century. The balance has already swung in favour of Miss Nightingale after a period of neglect, weighted down by the call for political correctness in the mid-twentieth century. This is confirmed by the steady rise in visitors from all over the world – 32,000 in 2006, including many parties of schoolchildren – to the Florence Nightingale Museum, situated on the site of St Thomas' Hospital in London where she established the first training school for nurses in 1860.

Over the years many myths and misunderstandings have been associated with Florence Nightingale's name, mostly without lasting effect. It may be useful to consider two of the more persistent rumours.

First, there was the belief that after the Crimean War she became a hypochondriac, dosing on opium, spending long hours on her couch and driving her colleagues to the point of exhaustion or death with overwork. There is an element of truth in this contention. She was a woman haunted by the memory of the endless lines of wounded and dying men in the corridors in the Scutari hospital, and vowed in a private note: *"I stand at the altar of the murdered men and while I live I fight their cause".* Florence Nightingale returned to England exhausted by the long voyage and still suffering from the after-effects of a severe attack of Crimean fever during the months May to August 1855. A photograph dated circa 1858 in the Claydon House collection – reproduced on a panel in the Florence Nightingale Museum – shows her still painfully thin, with drawn face and limp hair. The fever (now believed to be chronic brucellosis) returned to plague her with physical symptoms until she was well into her sixties, and opium may have been used as a tranquiliser.

When the illness struck, her medical adviser and friend, Dr Sutherland, would send her to a nursing home in Malvern to recuperate.

Against the advice of her friends, and within a few weeks of returning to England, she began campaigning for the British army at home with the slogan *"Our soldiers enlist to die in barracks",* working long into the night with Sidney Herbert and their "kitchen cabinet". In spite of opposition from the Minister of War, Lord Panmure – christened "the Bison" by Miss Nightingale – a Royal Commission was set up in 1858.

There is recurring criticism of Florence Nightingale's

treatment of the Jamaican nurse, Mary Seacole, widely celebrated for her work at Balaclava during the Crimean War and hailed as an icon for black children. She was born in Kingston, Jamaica, in about 1805 (the actual date is uncertain) of a British soldier and a Jamaican mother, who practised the art of herbal medicine and taught her daughter all she knew. In 1854, in her late forties, Mary, already well-travelled and widowed, was distressed by reports of the terrible sufferings of the British troops in the Crimea, and travelled to London hoping to find sponsorship for a journey to the Crimea where she could use her skills to help the wounded.

When Mary Seacole learned that Miss Nightingale was authorized by the War Office to take a party of nurses to the Crimea, she endeavoured to make contact with Sidney Herbert, but was referred to his residence, where she received a message from Mrs Herbert that the nurses had already left for Istanbul. In her autobiography, *The Wonderful Adventures of Mrs Seacole in Many Lands*, she reports that on hearing this news she burst into tears, but eventually found a sponsor and set off for the Crimea. The colour of her skin was immaterial to the outcome of her efforts to join Florence Nightingale.

Her arrival at the Scutari Hospital coincided with a surge of wounded men from the Battle of the Alma: the nurses were under huge pressure, but Florence Nightingale found time for a meeting with her and managed to find her a bed for the night before Mrs Seacole continued her journey across the Black Sea to Balaclava. There this indomitable woman set up the British Hotel on the road from the battlefields, providing much needed comfort, food and drink, and treatment of their wounds for weary soldiers fresh from the horrors of war.

Their paths crossed again when the war ended in 1856 and both returned to England. Mrs Seacole received many tributes from army personnel and was granted a pension. She hoped to obtain a hospital post and asked Miss Nightingale to supply a testimonial, but her request was refused on the grounds that she lacked formal nursing training. In private, however, Miss Nightingale was critical of the lax standards of behaviour in the British Hotel.

The nurses under Miss Nightingale's control in the Crimean hospitals were strictly disciplined; those found guilty of misbehaviour were sent back to England forthwith. The Register of Nurses held in the Florence Nightingale Museum gives details of their misdemeanours together with pithy comments from Miss Nightingale. Although a formidable disciplinarian, she was a sensitive and caring woman. Shortly after her arrival at Scutari she wrote a long letter to Sidney Herbert detailing appalling sanitary conditions and shortages of basic equipment which must be tackled, and mentioning the difficulty in finding one or two workmen to carry out improvements necessary *to get in a few poor soldiers' wives into our little lying-in hospital.* Another priority was the provision of screens to shield the patients from the grisly sight of amputations being performed without anaesthetics, faced with the realization that it would be their turn the following day. While empathising with human suffering, Florence Nightingale had the ability to find practical solutions for the alleviation of pain. She was not only a nurse, but a superb administrator.

These two remarkable but very different women deserve high praise for their work in the Crimea, but any attempt to compare one with the other can only serve to diminish their achievements.

From time to time attacks on Florence Nightingale erupt in the press following the discovery of some small nugget of unpublished material. The sale at a London auction house in September 2007 of a notebook with copies of letters from the Medical Inspector-General in the Crimea, Dr John Hall, to his superiors in the War Office, is a case in point. Dr Hall complained bitterly about Miss Nightingale's conduct in the Crimea, calling her "a petticoat *imperieuse* in the Medical *imperio*". This comes as no great revelation; it is recorded by Cook in Volume I of his biography and was fully covered in the Report of the Royal Commission in 1857, where facts and figures showed that *"the health of the Army . . . was shamefully sacrificed by official neglect"*. In a letter to Lord Raglan, the commander of the forces in the Crimea, Sidney Herbert wrote *"I cannot help feeling that Dr Hall resents offers of assistance as being slurs on his preparations."*

When Florence Nightingale and her party of thirty-eight nurses arrived at the Barrack Hospital in Scutari (a former Turkish barracks) on 24 November 1854, Dr Hall made every effort to prevent their direct involvement with the wounded. Male nurses and orderlies were forbidden to work with Miss Nightingale. During this period she remained quietly aloof in her tower, setting the nurses to work on making bandages. When they became restless she quelled them with the threat *the strongest will be needed at the washtub*. After the battles of Alma, Balaclava and Inkerman the corridors of the Barrack Hospital were overflowing with casualties; by 23 December the number had risen to 2,434. Florence Nightingale estimated that there were four miles of beds and not eighteen inches apart. Many of the doctors welcomed the trained nurses, but the battle with Dr Hall dragged on, particularly on the issue of access to essential supplies and the need to provide nourishing food for the patients.

The purchase of Dr Hall's notebook by the Wellcome Trust for £4,000 was widely publicised. A full-page spread in *The Guardian* on 3 September 2007 led with a provocative headline *"Angel of mercy or power-crazed meddler?"*; it was followed on 4 September 2007 with a long article in the *Daily Mail* with a strangely similar headline. The letters throw no new light on the relationship between Dr Hall and "The Lady with the Lamp".

By contrast, the discovery of an unrecorded photograph taken by professional photographers, William Frost and William Slater of Romsey in 1858, aroused widespread interest and brought a stream of visitors to the Florence Nightingale Museum. The sepia print was found in an old album (one of three with photographs of prominent residents in the Romsey area of Hampshire) and is now in the possession of the Florence Nightingale Museum Trust.

There is a striking difference between obligatory photographs of Florence Nightingale taken after the Crimean War showing a grave, slender woman in a simple black gown and this charmingly romantic image. Florence is seated on a flight of steps in the grounds of the Nightingale home, Embley Park (now a boys' public school), with a tall sculpted stone vase in the background, which can still be found in the garden. She is wearing an elegant gown with a widely spread ruched skirt and is intent on a book. At the time Florence would have been thirty-eight years of age.

From this photograph it is possible to evoke an image of a younger Florence – the shy seventeen-year-old girl who went with her family on a grand tour of Europe in 1837. She kept a meticulous record of their journey through France, Northern Italy and Switzerland, with comments on social conditions and politics. She enjoyed picnics and court balls, and revelled in the art and music, particularly opera at La Scala, Milan, describing herself as *"music-mad"*. There was an amusing incident at a ball in Genoa: *"my partner and I made an embrouillement, and a military officer came up with a very angry face to challenge me for having refused him and then not dancing."*

On their homeward journey the Nightingale family spent the winter of 1838 in Paris, where Florence was taken up by Mary Clarke and introduced to her brilliant salon patronised by many of the leading French intellectuals. This charming woman, of half-Irish and half Scottish descent,

became a close friend and regular correspondent; Florence was always sure of a warm welcome by "Clarkey" and her circle whenever she could escape to Paris.

In 1844 an American visitor, Julia Ward Howe, and her husband, Dr Howe, were entertained at Embley. Florence was then twenty-four years of age and Mrs Howe later wrote in her *Reminiscences 1819–99: "Florence was rather elegant than beautiful; she was tall and graceful of figure, her countenance mobile and expressive, her conversation most interesting."* A pencil sketch of Florence a year earlier (circa 1843) by her cousin, Hilary Bonham Carter, is reproduced in the first volume of Edward Cook's biography.

Hilary Bonham-Carter's drawing of the young Florence Nightingale

rence Nightingale photographed in the garden at Embley

During the next ten years, despite being surrounded by a lively circle of loving friends and relations, having a full social life, and travelling abroad with Charles and Selina Bracebridge, Florence Nightingale became increasingly restless and depressed. She found it difficult to conform to the pattern of Victorian family life and longed to be of use to suffering humanity, possibly as a hospital nurse – but her mother was horrified when the subject was broached.

There was, however, a deeper reason for her unhappiness. During the 1840s she had met Richard Monckton Milnes, a friend through the Nightingales' Derbyshire connections. They were mutually attracted and it seems from a biography of Monckton Milnes by I W Reid that he courted Florence for seven years. He was a handsome man, well-connected (created Baron Houghton in 1863) and a gifted poet – in fact highly eligible – but she, though clearly in love, found it impossible to accept his repeated offers of marriage. In an autobiographical note, one of many preserved from this period of her life, Florence attempted to analyse her emotions: "*I have an intellectual nature which requires satisfaction and that would find it in him. I have a 'passional' nature which requires satisfaction, and that would find it in him. I have a moral, an active nature which requires satisfaction, and that would not find it in his life. I can hardly find satisfaction for any of my natures. Sometimes I think I will satisfy my 'passional' nature at all events, because that will at least secure me from the evil of dreaming. But would it? I could not satisfy this nature by spending a life with him in making society and arranging domestic things . . ."* And therein lay the rub, but there can be no doubt of the depth of her anguish in making the decision to go her own way. In 1850 she wrote in her diary on her birthday: *"I am 30, the age at which Christ began His mission. Now no more childish things, no more love, no more marriage. Now, Lord, let me only think of Thy will."*

Richard Monckton Milnes (1809–85) married the Honourable Annabella Hungerford Crewe in 1851, but continued throughout his life to follow the paths and peaks of Florence Nightingale's extraordinary career. He was always ready – in the role of family friend – to give his support and she often turned to him for advice. But the unremitting pain caused by her refusal to share his life is evident in the brief letter sent on the eve of her departure for the Crimea (18 October 1854): "My dear Friend, I hear you are going to the East, and I am happy it is so, for the good you will do there . . . You can undertake *that*, when you could not undertake me. God bless you, dear Friend, wherever you go." Florence Nightingale has been criticized for her somewhat controversial views on marriage. She recognized that for most women of her generation the married state – even if it fell short of the ideal – was their proper lot in life. On the other hand she thought some women were marked out for the single life. She believed there was a need to find new spheres of usefulness for all women, whether married or single.

Florence Nightingale had many women friends and relatives with whom she corresponded. Her personal

Richard Monckton
Milnes

letters are caring, amusing, with snippets of gossip; sometimes sentimental in the Victorian style. To her nurses in the training school at St Thomas' Hospital she wrote an annual letter of encouragement and reached out to those who, once qualified, took up posts as matrons as far afield as Liverpool, Edinburgh, Sydney and Philadelphia.

She also enjoyed the friendship of many eminent men – partly a meeting of minds, as with Sidney Herbert, but deepening to real affection as the relationship continued. For example, Colonel Sir Henry Yule first met Miss

Nightingale in his official capacity as a member of the India Office Sanitary Committee. The strength of their friendship can be judged from a letter he wrote in 1889: "As long as I live, but I am not counting on that as a long period, it will be a happiness to think that I was brought into communication with you."

Dr John Sutherland was sent to the Crimea in 1855 as head of a Sanitary Commission. After the war he collaborated with Florence Nightingale on the campaign for the health of the army in India and became her chief "sanitarian" as well as her personal medical adviser. His wife reported that on his death bed in 1891 he roused himself sufficiently to read a letter from Miss Nightingale and almost his last words were "Give her my love and blessing".

In lighter vein, Dr J Croft, one of the surgeons at St Thomas' Hospital and for many years medical instructor to the Nightingale probationers, wrote in February 1873: "I have always dreaded remaining a stagnant man. I hope to become, as you would have me, an active and faithful comrade." And again, on resigning his post, expressed the pleasure he had found in working under "so lovable and adorable a leader as Miss Nightingale".

To give one more example, Mr William Rathbone, a Liverpool philanthropist, sought Florence Nightingale's advice on the introduction of a system of district nursing for the poor of Liverpool and entered into a long correspondence with her. On her birthday in May 1865 he wrote begging to be allowed to provide a flower-stand

for her room and keep it supplied with flowers – "If the plants will only flourish, as the good seed you have planted here is doing, they will be bright enough." What magic did this extraordinary woman possess? As a colleague she could be demanding and at times infuriating, but she seldom raised her voice, using humour and charm to ease a difficult situation and win her case. The affection she aroused was always at the root of these relationships.

The friendship with Benjamin Jowett was certainly the most enduring. Edward Cook writes "No man knew her for so many years as Mr Jowett." In 1893 Benjamin Jowett became very ill and on 18 September dictated his last letter to Miss Nightingale: "Fare you well. How greatly am I indebted to you for all your affection. How large a part has your life been of my life. There is only time I think for a few words."

All these important friendships covering so many years of her life must have given Florence Nightingale great comfort, as did the letters she received from her beloved Crimean Veterans to whom she wrote annually. In a letter to Samuel Smith dated 22 October 1861 she commented on a letter from one a veteran who would "willingly offer his hand and heart which are free, only you are so much above me" by remarking *"it is gratifying to observe that this is not the first fruits of my Veterans' letter – and that I could have as many husbands as Mahomet's mother"*. Today, as the Indian nation surges ahead to play a leading role in the world, the number of its people living below the poverty line

portrait of Florence Nightingale in 1887

represents one quarter of the total population of 1.1 billion, and of these the majority are the rural poor. It seems that in over a century little has changed and it must be hoped that new voices will soon be raised to bring about an improved standard of living for these unfortunate people for whom Florence Nightingale fought so valiantly.

Envoi

Benjamin Jowett

Quotation from a letter dated 11 December 1879 from Benjamin Jowett, Master of Balliol College, Oxford.

"There was a great deal of romantic feeling about you twenty-three years ago when you came home from the Crimea. And now you work on in silence, and nobody knows how many lives are saved by your nurses in hospitals . . . ; how many soldiers who would have fallen victim to bad air, bad water, bad drainage and ventilation, are now alive owing to your forethought and diligence; how many natives of India (they might be counted probably by hundreds of thousands) in this generation and in generations to come have been preserved from famine and oppression and the load of debt by the energy of a sick lady who can scarcely rise from her bed. The world does not know all this or think about it. But I know it and often think about it.

Preface

The report of the Royal Commissioners on the sanitary condition of the Indian army was signed on May 19th, 1863. The following short abstract of some of the leading principles in that Report was read at the Edinburgh meeting of the Social Science Association held in October of the same year. It is now reprinted in consequence of many applications made for copies, on the ground that the paper had been found useful for soldiers and others interested in the Indian health question. Since the inquiry of the Royal Commission was begun, several great measures advocated in the Report and urged in the following pages, have been carried out. A Commission of Health has been appointed for each Presidency. And one of these Commissions, that for Bengal, has given public evidence of the zeal with which it has entered on its work. These authorities have been put into communication with the

Barrack and Hospital Improvement Commission at the War Office, which now contains members representing the India Government. And by this time the India Commissions have been put in possession* of all the more recent results of sanitary works and measures which have been of use at home.

The military authorities in India have also been actively engaged in improving the soldier's condition. And several of the worst personal causes of ill-health to which the soldier was in former times exposed have been or are being removed. The introduction of soldiers' gardens, trades, and workshops, which was begun in India a number of years since, has seen its happy results. The men have begun to find out that it is better to work than to sleep and to drink, even during the heat of the day.

One regiment marching into a station, where cholera had been raging for two years, were "chaffed" by the regiments marching out, and told they would never come out of it alive. The men of the entering battalion answered, they would see; we won't have cholera, they think. And they made gardens with such good effect that they had the pleasure, not only of eating their own vegetables, but of being paid for them too by the Commissariat. And this in a soil which no regiment had been able to cultivate before. And not a man had cholera. These good soldiers fought against disease, too, by work-shops and gymnasia.

At all the hill stations the men have covered the whole

hill-sides with their gardens. Government gives prizes to the best gardeners. And means of employment and occupation for the troops are being everywhere extended.

As for trades, I have seen the balance-sheets of 82 battalions of infantry, and of five regiments of cavalry in Bengal, for six months ending June, 1863; and these brave fellows are actually making money. The wages paid to men for working in the half-year were £28,237.

The balance from preceding half-year	£8,203
Amount realised for work last six months	£55,426
Value of stock on hand	£17,216
	£75,845

That this money goes not to canteen or bazaar is shown by the savings banks. One battalion returning to England took £7,000 with it in its savings bank. Of 26 other infantry regiments, none had less than £3,000, nine had £4,000, five had £5,000 and up to £6,000 in theirs.

But want of accommodation in barracks for workshops has, alas, fettered this great progress.

At gymnastics the men get strength to bear the heat, though Highland regiments cannot quite rival themselves at games in the Highlands. The men are paraded for gymnastics at first, but like the exercise so much that they continue it of their own accords. Again, however, want of cover for gymnasia in barracks puts a stop to what otherwise might be done.

Cricket is general; fives, single-stick, and other manly games are common.

In short, work and all kinds of exercise cause sickly men to flourish. One regiment, sick of scurvy, and not recovering even at one of the healthiest stations, was cured by working at a mountain road in the rains, with only temporary huts for shelter.

Soldiers' libraries are everywhere supplied by Government. Bengal regiments generally manage to have some kind of reading-room; but reading rooms specially constructed for their object are few.

Better cook-houses, cleaner cooking, are being introduced; and soldiers are taught to cook.

In the mean time, the regulation two drams have been reduced to one. The one dram is to be diluted with water. A Legislative Act imposes a heavy fine or imprisonment on the illicit sale of spirits near cantonments. Government supplies good beer, and plenty of it. Where there are recreation rooms, refreshments (prices all marked) are spread on a nice clean table. This the men like very much. And decrease in drink may be very much attributed to increase of useful work and of play, as the Commander-in-Chief in India himself says.

The practical result of these reforms is, then, that the soldier's time is more profitably occupied than formerly and that intemperance and crime have visibly diminished.

So far for the soldier's habits. But the main causes of disease in India, want of drainage, want of water-supply, for stations and to~ want of proper barracks and hospitals, remain as before in all their primitive perfection. Of this there is no doubt.

The above-mentioned improvements have removed several of the causes of disease enumerated in the Report of the Royal Commission. And they have also, happily, taken away some of the point in this paper.

Nevertheless it has been thought best to reprint it as read, because there are stations where little or nothing has been done in improving the soldier's habits, and because the great work of civilization in India has yet to be begun. It is moreover to be feared that little amendment has taken place in the self-indulgent eating and drinking habits of the European population, generally.

While thankfully acknowledging the excellent beginning made, since the advent to power of the present noble Governor-General of India, enough remains to justify this reprint.

F N

August, 1864

Appendix A (Chapter 1)

HOW PEOPLE MAY LIVE AND NOT DIE IN INDIA.

A meeting of the Social Science Association is surely the place to discuss one of the most important of social questions, viz., how the British race is to hold possession of India; and to bestow upon its vast populations the benefit of a higher civilisation.

The first part of the question is for the present the most important. For, if it be impossible to keep possession of the country, there is an end of the problem.

The Royal Commission on the sanitary state of the army in India, whose two folio volumes of report and appendix constitute a new social starting point for Indian civilisation has shown that, unless the health of British troops in India can be improved, and the enormous death-rate reduced, this country will never be able to hold India with a British army.*

---

* This report, unlike other reports, was based on two kinds of evidence ; 1. The usual oral evidence of witnesses: 2. Reports from every station in India, in answer to printed questions sent out, the answers being signed by the commanding officer, the engineer office, and the medical officer of each station. It was truly said that such a complete picture of the life in India, both British and native, is contained in no other book in existence.

The time has not yet arrived for the pressure of the death-rate it discloses to be fully experienced, because the present large army is comparatively new to the country. But, unless active measures are taken by the India Government and by the military authorities to give effect to the recommendations of the Commission, it is unhappily certain that the mortality will increase with the length of service. And then will be felt the difficulty stated by Sir Alexander Tulloch, viz, of filling up the ranks of those, prematurely slain by preventible disease, from the recruiting depots at home. Few men have had so much experience in this department of the Service. And he tells us that he very much doubts whether an army of seventy thousand men can be kept up in India, with the present death-rate.

In former times, when the company's troops bore but a small proportion to the resources (in men) of this country, the death-rate was not so much felt. The small army was swept away; and, its place supplied, as often as necessary, from the recruiting offices at home. But, now that a large proportion of the whole British army is stationed in India, the question whether we shall hold or lose India will depend very much on the steps taken to protect it from disease.

The statement that the average death-rate of troops, serving in India, was no less than 69 per 1,000 per annum, took the country by surprise.

The accuracy of the average could not be denied, because the statement was made on the authority of Sir Alexander Tulloch, and confirmed by a separate inquiry made with the help of the Registrar General's Office, at the request of the Commission.

But it was endeavoured to explain away the obvious result of the figures, by showing that the average was not constant – that, in certain years and groups of years, the death-rate was much greater than in others; that the mortality in the years of excess was due to wars or other causes; that peace, and not sanitary measures, was there-fore the remedy. And, in short, that the statement of a death-rate, avenging 69 per 1,000 per annum, was not a fair representation of the case.

To this there is the simple reply that, during this present century, there has been an average loss, from death alone, of 69 men out of every 1,000 per annum – it matters not how the mortality has been distributed – that there is every reason to believe that, if things go on as they have done in this present century, we shall go on losing our troops at the rate of 30, 50, 70, 90,

100 and upwards, per 1,000. And all the arithmetic in the world cannot conceal the fact that the law, by which men perish in India under existing sanitary negligence, is 69 per 1,000 per annum; this death-rate is, in fact, understated, for it says nothing of the invalids sent home from India who die at sea, or within a short time of their arrival at home; nor of the loss to the service by destroyed health; nor of the mutiny years. It takes into account only those who die in India, and in the ordinary course of service.

Few people have an idea of what a death-rate of 69 per 1,000 represents-the amount of inefficiency from sickness-Of invaliding.

Assuming the strength of the Indian army at 73,000 British troops – and taking the death-rate at present alone, without the sickness and invalids in such an army, with this present death-rate, will lose, on an average of years, an entire brigade of 5,037 men per annum. It may lose, some years, half that number. But, in other years, it will lose two such brigades.

And where are we to find 10,000 recruits to fill up the gap of deaths of a single unhealthy year?

It is said that the death-rates of the war-years being the highest (not from wounds), peace, and not sanitary"measures, is the remedy. As well might it be said that the British army, having nearly perished before Sevastopol, not from wounds, but from want of every supply of civilised life, peace, and not the supply of the wants of civilised life, was the remedy.

The Royal Commission has shown that, if the death-rate were reduced to even twenty per thousand per annum (which is too high), i.e., double that of home stations, since these stations were improved, to India would be saved a tax equal to £1,000 sterling per diem; and this represents the mere cost of replacing the men cut off by excess of premature and preventible mortality.

1. Unofficial people are everywhere asking the question, how this great death-rate has arisen – how it happens that one of the most civilised and healthy nations in the world no sooner lands the pick of its working population in tropical climates (for similar losses occur in all tropical climates among us) than they begin to die off at this enormous rate.

I am afraid the reply must be that British civilisation is insular and local, and that it takes small account of how the world goes on out of its own island. There is a certain aptitude amongst other nations which enables them to adapt themselves, more or less, to foreign climates and countries. But, wherever you place your Briton, you may feel quite satisfied that he will care nothing about climates.

If he has been a large eater and a hard drinker at home ten to one he will be, to say the least of it, as large an eater and as hard a drinker in the burning plains of Hindustan. Enlist an Irish or a Scotch labourer who has done many a hard day's work, almost entirely on farinaceous or vegetable diet, with an occasional dose of whiskey, place him at some Indian station where the thermometer ranges at between 90° and 100°, and he will make no difficulty in disposing of three or four times the quantity of animal food he ever ate under the hardest labour during winters at home – if, indeed, he ever ate any at all.

Now the ordinary system of dieting British soldiers in India is more adapted to a cold climate than that of out-door farm servants doing work in England.

More than this, the occasional dram at home is commuted, by regulation, in India into a permission to drink two drams, i.e., 6 oz. of raw spirits every day. And be it remembered that, at the same time, the men have little or nothing to do. The craving for spirits, induced by this regulation habit of tippling, leads to increase of drunkenness – so that, what with over-eating, over-drinking, total idleness, and vice springing directly from these, the British soldier in India has small chance indeed of coping with the climate, so-called. The regulation-allowance of raw spirit which a man may obtain at the canteen is no less than 18½ gallons per annum; which is, I believe, three times the amount per individual which has raised Scotland, in the estimation of economists, to the rank of being the most spirit-consuming nation in Europe. Of late years, malt liquor has been partly substituted for spirits. But, up to the present time, every man, if he thinks fit, may draw his 184 gallons a year of spirits, besides what he gets sure repetitiously at the Bazaar

Tippling is unfortunately not confined to common soldiers. Officers also use spirits, generally brandy with water or with soda-water. It relieves exhaustion for the time at the expense of the constitution, and is a prime agent in sending officers to the hills to recover their health and home on sick furlough. The practice is at some stations called "pegging" alluding to putting pegs in one's coffin. Is not this practice of "pegging" one reason why officers are less healthy in India than civilians.

So much for intemperance. But not to this alone, nor to this mainly, nor to this and its kindred vice together, is to be laid the soldier mortality in India.

The diseases from which the soldier mainly suffers there are miasmatic: now intemperance never produced miasmatic diseases yet. They are foul-air diseases and foul-water diseases: fevers, dysenteries, and so on. But intemperance may cause liver disease; and it may put the man into a state of health which prevents him from resisting miasmatic causes.

2. What are these causes? We have not far to look.

The Briton leaves his national civilisation behind him, and brings his personal vices with him.

At home there have been great improvements everywhere in agricultural and in town drainage, and in providing plentiful and pure water supplies.

There is nothing of the kind in India. There is no drainage either in town or in country. There is not a single station drained. If such a state of things existed at home, we should know that we have fevers, cholera, and epidemics to expect. But hitherto only a few enlightened people have expected anything of the kind from these same causes in India (although they are always happening).

As regards water, there is certainly not a single barrack in India, which is supplied, in our sense of the term, at all. There are neither water-pipes nor drainpipes. Water is to be had either from tanks, into which all the filth on the neighbouring surface may at any time be washed by the rains; or from shallow wells, dug in unwholesome or doubtful soil. So simple a piece of mechanism as a pump is unknown. Water is drawn in skins, carried in skins on the backs of men or bullocks, and poured into any sort of vessels in the barracks for use. The quantity of water is utterly insufficient for health, and as to the quality, the less said about that, the better. There is no reason to hope that any station has what in this country would be called a pure water supply. And at some it is to be feared that, when men drink water, they drink cholera with it.

The construction of barracks, where men have to pass their whole period of service, is another illustration of how completely home civilisation is reversed in India. All our best soldiers have been brought up in country cottages. And when in barracks at home, there are rarely more than from twelve to twenty men in a room. But as soon as the soldier comes to India he is put into a room with 100, or 300, and, in one case, with as many as 600 men. Just when the principle of sub-division into a number of detached barracks becomes of, literally, vital importance, the proceeding is reversed. And the men are crowded together under circumstances certain, even in England to destroy their health.

To: take, illustration :-Our home British population is about the most active in the world. In fact we in this country consider exercise and health inseparable; but as soon as the same men go to India, they are shut up all day in their hot, close barrack-rooms, where they also eat and sleep; they are not allowed to take exercise; all their meals are eaten in the hottest part of the day, and served to them by native servants ; and they lie on their beds idle and partly sleeping till sunset! "Unrefreshing day-sleep" is indeed alleged as one of the causes for the soldier's ill-health in India – the soldier, the type of endurance and activity, who now becomes the type of sloth!

3. The Indian social state of the British soldier is not only the reverse of the social state of the soldier at home, and of the class from which he is taken; but there is a great exaggeration in the wrong direction. Yet people are surprised that British soldiers die in India; and they lay the whole blame on the climate.

It is natural to us to seek a scapegoat for every

neglect, and climate has been made to play this part ever since we set foot in India. Sir Charles Napier says, "That every evil from which British troops have suffered has been laid at its door." "The effects of man's imprudence are attributed to climate; if a man gets drunk the sun has given him a headache, and so on." In regard to Delhi, he says, "Every garden, if not kept clean, becomes a morass; weeds flourish, filth runs riot and the grandest city in India has the name of being insalubrious, although there is nothing evil about it that does not appear to be of man's own creation."

One most important result of the inquiry of the Royal Commission has been to destroy this bugbear. They have reduced "climate" to its proper dimensions and influence, and they have shown that, just as hot moist weather at home calls people to account for sanitary neglects and acts of intemperance, so does the climate of India call to account the same people there. There is not a shadow of proof that India was created to be the grave of the British race. The evidence, on the contrary, is rather in the other direction, and shows that all that the climate requires is that men shall adapt their social habits and customs to it; as, indeed, they must do to the requirements of every other climate under heaven.

This necessity includes all the recommendations made by the Royal Commission for improving the health, and reducing to one-sixth the death-rate of

the British army in India. They all amount to this :-
You have in India such and such a climate; if you
wish to keep your health in it:-

Be moderate in eating and drinking; eat very little
animal food; let your diet be chiefly farinaceous and
vegetable.

Spirits are a poison, to be used only (like other
poisons) for any good purpose, under medical
advice.

Use beer or light wine, but sparingly.

Drink coffee or tea.

Clothe yourself lightly to suit the climate, wearing
thin flannel always next the skin.

Take plenty of exercise, and use prudence and
common sense as to the times of it.

So far for personal habits. But a man cannot drain
and sewer his own city, nor lay a water supply on to
his own station, nor build his own barracks. What
follows pertains to Government

Let it be the first care to have a plentiful supply
of pure water laid on for every purpose.

Drain all dwellings.

Have no cess-pits.

Attend rigidly to cleansing, not only to surface
cleansing.

Never build in a wet hollow nor on a sludgy river-
bank, which would be avoided by sensible people
even at home.

Never crowd large numbers into the same room;

Build separate barrack-rooms, instead of large barracks.

Place these so that the air plays freely round them.

Raise them above the ground with a current of air beneath.

Do these things, and the climate may be let to take care of itself.

But, if we would make India about as healthy as England, only somewhat hotter, let us have improved agriculture and agricultural drainage.

If all these improvements were carried out the normal death-rate of the British soldier would be not 69 per 1,000, but 10 per 1,000, say the Commissioners.

But it is not for the soldier alone we speak. The report has a much deeper meaning and intent than this :- it aims at nothing less than to bring the appliances of a higher civilisation to the natives of India. Such revelations are made, especially in the reports from the stations, with regard to the sanitary condition of these, as to be almost incredible. Everywhere the people are suffering from epidemic diseases; fevers, dysenteries, cholera – constant epidemics we may call them, and constant high death rates (how high can never be known, because there is no registration).

The plague and pestilence is the ordinary state of things. The extraordinary is when these sweep over large tracts, gathering strength in their course, to pass over gigantic mountain ranges and to spread their ravages over Western Asia and Europe. And all this might be saved!

We know the causes of epidemic outbreaks here. Take the worst condition of the worst and most neglected town district at home.; and this is, to say the least of it, much better than the normal condition of nearly the whole surface of every city and town in India.

Not one city or town is drained.

Domestic filth round the people's houses is beyond description.

Water-supply is from wells, or tanks, in ground saturated with filth.

No domestic conveniences.

Every spare plot of ground is therefore in a condition defying as to mention it farther.

Rains of the rainy season wash the filth of the past dry season into the wells and tanks.

The air in, and for some distance round, native towns is as foul as sewer air. [At Madras a wall has actually been built to keep this from the British town.]

No sanitary administration. No sanitary police.

Here then we have, upon a gigantic scale, the very conditions which invariably precede epidemics at home. India is the focus of epidemics. Had India not been such, cholera might never have been. Even now, the Sunderbunds, where every sanitary evil is to be found in its perfection, are nursing a form of plague increasing yearly in intensity, covering a larger and larger area, and drawing slowly round the capital of India itself.

Are we to learn our lesson in time?

Some say :- What have we to do with the natives or their habits?

Others find an excuse for doing nothing in the questions arising out of caste. But caste has not interfered with railways.

The people: of themselves have no power to prevent or remove these evils – which now stand as an impassable barrier against all progress. Government is everything in India.

The time has gone past when India was considered a mere appendage of British commerce. In holding India, we must be able to show the moral right of our tenure. Much is being done, no doubt, to improve the country – by railways, canals, and means of communication; to improve the people by education, including under this word, European literature and science.

But what at home can be done in education, if we neglect physical laws? How does education progress here, without means of cleanliness, of decency, or health? The school lessons of a month are sapped in an hour. If the people are left a prey to epidemics and to immoral agencies in their homes, it is not much good sending them to school. Where should we be now with all our schools, if London were like Calcutta, Madras, or Bombay ?-the three seats of Government in India.

The next great work then is sanitary reform in India. There is not a town which does not want –

Water-supply.
Draining.
Paving.
Cleansing.

Healthy plans for arranging and constructing buildings.

Together with agricultural drainage and improved cultivation all round.

These things the people cannot do for themselves.

But the India Government can do them. And, in order to do them, three Health Departments (one for each of the Presidencies) have been recommended by the Royal Commission, together with a Home Commission to help these Departments in bringing the appliances of a better civilisation to India.

The work is urgent. Every day it is left undone adds its quota of inefficiency to the British Army, and its thousands of deaths to the native population. Danger is common to European and to native. Many of the best men this country ever had have fallen victims to the same causes of disease which have decimated the population of Hindustan. And so it will be till the India Government has fulfilled its vast responsibility towards those great multitudes who are no longer strangers and foreigners, but as much the subjects of our beloved Queen as any one of us.

The real, the main point in the Report of the Royal Commission is this:

Look to the state of your stations first then look to the hills for help. Your stations and cities are in a condition which, in the finest temperate climate in Europe, would have been the cause of the Great Plague of half the population being swept off by disease. And on the other hand, no climate in the world, certainly not that of India, could kill us, if we did not kill ourselves by our neglects. We complain of the climate, when the wonder is that there is one of us left, under a sky which certainly intensifies causes of disease – so much so indeed that, one would have thought, it might set men to work to remove these causes, and twice as vigorously as in a temperate climate, instead of not at all.

But no: our cities are not those of civilised men.

It cannot now be said, as Burke did: "England has built no bridges, made no high roads, cut no navigations." But in all that regards the social improvement of cities, still it must be said, as he did-how many years ago ?" Were we driven out of India this day, nothing would remain to tell that it had been possessed, during the inglorious period of our dominion, by anything better than the ourang-outang, or the tiger."

For how much is it better now?

Bring your cities and stations within the pale of civilisation. As they are, they are the life destroyers, not the climate.

The hills, those very climates to which you look for succour, are becoming so pestiferous from your neglects, that they bear out this indictment. They cry to you is we do: reform your stations-thence comes the deadly influence.

The question is no less one than this – How to create a public health department for India – how to bring a higher civilisation into India. What a work, what a noble task for a Government-no "inglorious period of our dominion" that, but a most glorious one!

That would be creating India anew. For God places His own power, His own life-giving laws in the hands of man. He permits man to create mankind by those laws – even as He permits man to destroy mankind by neglect of those laws.

Postscript

Since this Paper was read, the lower death-rate of troops new to the country has actually been put forward as a proof that India is becoming healthy, and the 69 per 1,000 is an old antiquated average! But more than this, the diminution of mortality arising from the short duration of service, is ascribed to improvements carried out at Indian stations since the Royal Commissioners began their inquiry. The leading authorities on the subject ascribe the vnstin causes of disease to want of drainage, bad sites, bad water badly distributed wretched sanitary condition of native bazaars and towns – bad barrack and bad hospital construction surface over-crowding from want of barrack accommodation-want of occupation for the men – intemperance in eating and drinking – want of proper barrack and hospital conveniences; it is difficult to see how India could have been freed from these causes of disease in three short years, which is about the average time since the Stational Reports were signed.

That something may have been done in the way of cleansing, ventilation, ablution, arraneinents, means of recreation, is possible.

But as to ventilation, it may almost he said that it is better to keep the foul air out than to let it iii, at least at certain stations of which we have reports up to nearly the latest date from India.

As to cleansing we have the report of a Government Commission on the last cholera, dated July 21, 1862, which tells us that, at a large station where cholera was fatal, the filth from the latrines was thrown down at places 100 yards from the barracks – that dead animals and every kind of refuse are accumulated in, the same places without burial that, before the cholera appeared, there were abominable cess-pools poisoning the whole atmosphere that neglect of the commonest principles of sanitary science favoured the epidemic that the filth from the native latrines was used for feeding sheep that, for all this, the local military authorities had not neglected "conservancy in any unusual degree," the reporters state-and that, bad as they considered it, the station was kept in much better order than niahat they had visited have also two printed document of the Public Works Department, dated Calcutta, June 26, and September 9, 1863, proving that the capital of India was in a much worse state than appeared from the Stational Report sent to the Royal Commission in June, 1860.

Appendix B (Chapter 11)

From the British Library (India Room), Guide to Sources for Science and the Environment

Extracts from reports relating to:
F – Urban Environments – Works of Improvement
I – Public Health and Sanitation
J – Military Health and Sanitation
S – Irrigation and Water Control
I – Public Health and Sanitation

(i) Madras Presidency

Improvements in the sanitary conditions and measures adopted for obtaining annual statements of the births and deaths throughout Madras 1856 1/F/4 2648 No 172311

Report of the Ootamund Improvement Committee 1861 L/E/3/737 No 12

Report on a project for the drainage of the town of Madras
H Tulloch 1865 V/27/842/9

Annual medical and sanitary report of Coorg, including reports
on civil dispensaries and vaccination 1877–99 V/24/3747

Report on the drainage of Madras W Clarke 1875
V/25/840/26–58

Madras Sanitary Commission Proceedings 1864–1900
V/25/840/26–58

Reports and orders of the Madras Government regarding the
adoption of the dry earth system of conservancy in barracks,
hospitals and prisons etc 1869 V/23/174/13

Memorandum on native latrines in the Madras Presidency
W Arnold Smith 1869 V/23/164/14

Further report and order of the Madras Government upon
the dry earth system of sewage in the Madras Presidency
1869 V123/175/15

Report on civil sanitation in the Presidency of Madras J L
Ranking 1869 V/27/840/27

Reports on the sanitary and other arrangements made during
fairs and festivals 1876–77 V/24/1461

(ii) Bombay Presidency

Correspondence on the subject of the drainage of Bombay
1863 V127/842/6

On the sanitary state of the city of Poona A H Leith and
T Martin 1864 V/23/233/79

On the sanitary state of the island of Bombay A H Leith 1864
V/23/233/80

Annual Report of the Director of Public Health for the Government of Bombay 1864–1920 V/24/3709–37

Report on the main drainage of Bombay R Aitken 1866
V/27/842/7

The drainage and sewage of Bombay H Tulloch 1872
V/27/842/8

Report on the working of the Contagious Diseases Act in Bombay 1883–88 V/24/2289

On the sanitary state of the city A H Leith and T Martin 1864 V/23/233/79

Proceedings of the Bombay Sanitary Commission 1865–73 V/27/842/6

Bombay Health Officer's Quarterly Report 1869–1920 V/25/840/13–24

(iii) United Provinces, Agra and Oudh

Sanitary Reports for Oudh 1868–76 V/24/382

Report on the treatment of sullage in the United Provinces G J Fowler 1864 V/27/842/17

Police and conservancy arrangements on the occasion of the late Hurdwar Fair 1867 L/PJ/3/1102 no 155

Sanitary summary of villages watered by the Western Jumna Canal 1867–69 A Taylor 1870 V/23/34016

Report on sanitary arrangements at the Gurmookhtesvar Fair C Planck 1868 V/23/128 Vol 2 no 1

(iv) Bengal Presidency

Relative to the prevalence of a very fatal epidemic in certain districts of the Nuddea and Burdwar divisions, progress of the epidemic with suggestions for the improvement of sanitary conditions in the area 1863 L/PJ/3/1 090 no 48

Report on the analysis of potable waters of cantonments in the Bengal Presidency 1866–71; reports on the water analysis in Bengal during 1866–67 and Dr Sheppard's special report on the analysis of the Delhi waters 1867 V/27/841/2

Scheme of analysis for use by medical officers on tour for the purpose of examining the potable waters of military and other stations [with additions, corrections and addenda] F N MacNamara [c1870] V/27/841/1 Reports on H Moule's dry earth conservancy scheme 1867 V/27/842/1

Report on the analysis of potable waters of cantonments in
the Bengal Presidency F N MacNamara 1868 V/27/841/2

Bengal public health report 1868–1920 V/24 3803–20

A short account of the modes of sewage disposal in some of
the chief towns of England, together with a little information on the subject likely to be of use in India T F Dowden
1869 V/27/842/2

Report on the drainage and conservancy of Calcutta D B
Smith 1869 V/27/842/2

Annual sanitary and medical report on the settlement of Port
Blair, Andamans 1869 V/24/3875

(v) Punjab

Sanitary improvements in the town of Akyab (Dr Archer states
that the chief cause of endemic diseases are geographical
and related position, imperfect drainage, diseased vegeta-
tion, impure water and food, imperfect ventilation and
crowded populations) 1845–47 F/4/2387 no 127295

(vi) Central Provinces

Annual public health report of the Central Provinces and Berar
1868–1920 V/24/3830–44

(vii) Burma

Report on the state of public health in Burma
1867–1920 V/24/3850–57

(viii) India

Report on sanitary measures in India 1868/69–1874/75
V/24/3862–63

Memorandum on measures adopted for sanitary improvement
in India up to the end of 1867, together with abstracts of
the sanitary reports hitherto forwarded from Bengal, Madras
and Bombay H L Anderson 1867 V/27/840/1

J – Military Health and Sanitation

India

Papers regarding the extent and nature of the sanitary establishments for the European troops in Bengal, Madras and Bombay Presidencies 1860 L/MiI/17/5/1995

Barrack and Hospital Improvement Commission – Suggestions in regard to sanitary works required for improving Indian stations 1864 V/27/843/1

Army Sanitary Commission – Remarks by the Sanitary Commission on the principles of construction for barracks for single and married men 1864 V/27/843/3

Rules regarding the measures to be adopted on the outbreak of cholera on appearance of smallpox 1870 V/27/853/5

Army Sanitary Commission – Suggestions in regard to sanitary works and measures required for improving Indian stations and their vicinity 1882 V/27/843/2

S. Irrigation and Water Control

Establishing control over India's water resources was a central objective in the drive of imperial science to organize nature and exploit its productivity. The records listed illustrate how, over the course of the nineteenth century, the relationship between land and water was comprehensively realigned according to new economic and political imperatives. These transformations demonstrate not only the manner in which the colonial state sought to physically order nature, but also acted as an important ideological justification for its governance.

This list documents the massive programme of engineering works by which the colonial authorities sought to exert control over the water resources of India. Attempts at hydraulic engineering in British India included a number of distinct activities, predominant among which was the building of canals and embankments whose primary (though often not sole) purpose was the provision of water for irrigation. Elsewhere we find attempts to improve water supply through water-boring and well irrigation. Drainage, flood control and hydro-electric schemes are other prominent interventions. Also detailed here are solutions to the problem of encroachment by the sea, efforts at erecting coastal defences and schemes for the reclamation of land. The common purpose of these works was to direct the movement of water, to lessen its destructive effects and to realise its powerful productive potential.

Alongside the documentation of engineering works, the India Office Records contain extensive material relating more broadly to the operation and administration of resulting projects. Administrative records defined how water was to be distributed, revenue generated, repairs carried out and disputes resolved. In these we see the formalisation of government control over the hydrological systems of South Asia.

India

Manuscript reports of a general nature about irrigation in India 1823–65 L/AG/47/I /121

Reports on Irrigation Works in India for the year 1875–76 L/E/5/69 no 36

Irrigation Works in India and Egypt (first edition) Robert Burton Buckley 1893 V/27/734/2

(i) Bengal

Papers of 1856, 1857 and 1858 on the Removal of the Damoodah Embankments etc V/23/97

Papers relating to Irrigation in Bengal [Damodah River] 1858 V/23/99

Irrigation works on the Damoodah River and at Mudoopore 1858 L/PWD/3/3 14 no 12

Operations to control the water of the Pugladeah River in Assam 1858 L/PWD/3/314 no 12

A project for Canals of Irrigation and Navigation from the River Soane in South Behar, CH Dickens 1861, 2 volumes Report V/27/733/26 Maps and plans V/27/733/27

Report on the Hidgellee Province Embankments, W D Short 1861 V/23/7 no **XXXVI**

Papers from 1859 to 1863 regarding the Damoodah Canal Project V/231/101 no **XL**

Reports of the East India Irrigation and Canal Company 1862–67, 121 volumes, from L/AG/37/1/1 through to L/AG/47/1/121

Papers from 1866 to 1870 regarding the Damoodah Canal Project V/23/103

Papers from 1897 to 1905 relating to the Tribeni Canal Project in the Champaran District V/23/108

(ii) Northern India

Report on the Drainage and Irrigation of the Terrain, CS Thomason 1864 V/27/842/16

Report on Measures to be taken in Remodelling the Ganges Canal, J Crofton 1864 V/27/842/16

Further papers regarding Irrigation from the Ootungun in Futtehpore, Sikri, Agra 1865 V/23/128 pp 265–339

Report of the Ganges Canal (Lawford) Committee 1866 – 3 volumes V/26/730/4 /5 /6

Extension of Canal Irrigation the Dehra Ismail Khan & Dehra Ghazee Khan Districts 1867 IOL ST 1530 no 18

Oudh: Sardah Canal and irrigation scheme, J G Forbes 1870 V/23/138

Oudh: Report on the Sardah Canal Project, J O Forbes 1871 V/27/733/19

Drainage and improvement of the Saharunpore and Moozuf-fernuggur Districts NWP 1871 V/23/130 vol VI

Katha Nuddee and the swamps in its Valley, report on its capacity for draining land west of the Eastern Jumna Canal 1872 V/23/I30 Vol VI

Papers connected with the Betwa Canal Project in the North-Western Provinces 1887 V/23/51 no CCXXXII

Failure of the Kali Nadi Aqueduct of the Lower Ganges Canal, correspondence from 1870 to 1887 V/23/52 no CCXL

Papers relating to the Construction of Wells for Irrigation in the North Western Provinces 1883 V/27/735/7

(iii) Orissa

Papers on the subject of the Cuttack rivers: including corre-spondence regarding the General State of the Embank-ments and Floods in the Pooree and Central Cuttack Districts 1860 V/23/99 pp 67355

Flood of 1855 as affecting the city of Cuttack and corre-spondence relative to the Control of the Mahanuddy River, J C Harris, W D Shirt and E A Samuells 1860 V/27/732/26

Reports of the East India Irrigation and Canal Company 1862–67 121 volumes, from L/AG/37/1/1 through to L/AG/47/1/121

Papers relating to the Orissa Coast Canal 1877–Si V/23146 no CCW

Papers relating to the Orissa Canals 1869 to 1877 and 1881 to 1883 V/23/105

Papers relating to the Orissa Coast Canal 1889 V/23/56 no CCLVII

(iv) South India

Report on the direct and indirect Effects of the Godavery and Krishna Annicuts in Rajahmundry and the Coleroon Anni-cuts in Tanjore and South Arcot 1858 V/27/732/4

Memorandum on the proposed Mauiy Tank, near Herioor, in Mysore, AT Cotton 1858 V/27/734/41

Report from the Collector of Tinnevelly on the occurrence of heavy floods in that District; urgent repairs to irrigation works 1870 L/E/3/757 no 9

Irrigation Works of the Kistna Delta, Madras 1873 V/27/730/8

Reports of the Madras Irrigation and Canal Company 1859–1880 9 volumes from L/AG/47/2/1 through to L/AG/47/2/9

Papers relating to the Buckingham Canal 1886 V/23/48 no CCXV

Papers connected with the Periar Irrigation Project in Madras Presidency 1886 V/23/48 no V/23/48 no CCXV

Papers relating to the Palar Anicut system in North Ascot 1886 V/23/49 no CCXIX

Papers relating to the Sangam Anicut project in Nellore District, A A G Malet 1890 V/23/58 no CCLXIX

The Engineering Works of the Godavari Delta: a descriptive and historical account, George T Walch 1896 V/27/732/11–12

History of the Buckingham Canal Project: with a descriptive account of the canal and its principal works and a guide to its future maintenance, A S Russell 1898 V/27/733/2

Note on Utilization of Water-Power, Periya Project 1898 V/27/740/47

History of the Periya Project, AT MacKenzie 1899 V/27/740/48

The engineering works of the Kistna Delta: a descriptive and historical account, George T Walch 1899 V/27/730/9 and V/27/730/10

Proposed construction of a Dam across the Sataree River 1859 L/PS/6/407 pp 299–304

Captain Chambers' report on the Irrigation from the Taptee River 1861 V/23/23 1

Report on the question of Irrigation in the Yerla Valley, A
Jacob 1864 V/23/234

Irrigation project for the Bombay Presidency: Land in the Paihra
and Godavery Valleys in the Ahmednuggur Collectorate (the
Lakh Project) 1866 V/23/332

A Paper on Irrigation in the Deccan and Southern V/23/332

Project for the Completion of an Ancient Unfinished Work
known as Bhatodee Tank in the Ahmednuggur Collectorate
of the Bombay presidency 1867 V/23/334

Papers relating to the Maynee Project in the Khuttaw Talooka
1867 V/23/334

Irrigation Projects for the Bombay Presidency: Tank at Erookh
near Sholapore 1867 2 volumes V/23/332 and V/23/333

Use of steam pumping machinery to raise water for irrigation in Khandeish District 1868 L/E13/520 no 51

Relief Works on the Neem River in the Indapoor and other
Talookas 1869 L/E13/853 no 38

Report on the Nira Canal Project, Poona District 1892
V/27/733/17

Report on Irrigation Works, Wells and Agricultural Works
in the Bombay Presidency and their relation to the protection of the country against Famine, H F Beale 1901 2
volumes: parts 1–3 V/27/734/13 part 4 and maps
V/27/734/14

Memorandum on Irrigation Works in the Bombay Presidency,
excluding Sindh, November 1901 M Visvesraya V/27/
734/1 S

(v) Western India

Sindh: modifications of the project for extension of a canal
beyond Hammerow on the Eastern Narra 1858 F/4/2713
no 195267

Irrigation in Sind: problems posed by the shifting channels of
the River Indus 1858 L/E/3/827 no 13

Papers relating to Canal irrigation in Sind with suggestions for its Improvement 1863 V/23/232 no LI

A Sketch of irrigation of Sindh, Robert Brunton 1867 V/27/734/19

Papers relating to the Mitrow Canal in the Eastern Narra District, Sindh 1867 V/23/334

Sindh: efforts adopted for controlling the water in the Western Narra 1868 L/E/3/849 no 33

Report connected with the Zhara Karez Irrigation Scheme, Baluchistan 1887 V/23/51 no CCXXXI

Papers relating to the Khushdil Khan Reservoir Scheme [Baluchistan] 1890 V/23/57 no CCLXIV

Report on the Jamrao Canal Project, Sind 1907 V/27/733/13

Sindh River Canal Project: estimate and Report, Henry Marsh 1907 V/27/733/20

(vi) Central India and Rajputana

Tank irrigation in the Districts of Ajrnere and Mhairwara, F Home 1868 V/23/128

(vii) North Western India

Embankment for protecting the Nowsheera Barracks from flood 1858 Ff412723 no 197600

Irrigation Canals, Shahpore District 1867 IOL ST 1530 no 10

Punjab: Application for Six of Norton's Tube Wells 1869 L/PS/6/566 no 190

Papers relating to the Sidhnai Canal Project in the Punjab 1883–84 V/23/53 no CCXLVIII

Correspondence relating to the construction of wells for irrigation 1886 TOR POS 5109 no 59

Papers relating to canals 1887 TOR POS 5109 no 62

Correspondence relating to the Ferozepur and Fazilka inundation canals 1887 TOR POS 5109 no 61

Papers relating to the irrigation works in the Sialkot District 1895 TOR POS 5111 no 71

Punjab Irrigation Branch Papers: Remodelling of Distribu-
taries on Old Canals, papers dated 1875–1904 V/25/734/28
no 10

(viii) Bombay and Bombay Presidency
Report on a Project for the Supply of Water to the Poona
Cantonment, P L Hart 1858 V/23/226 no XLVII
Correspondence on the Subject of the Drainage of Bombay
1863 V/27/842/6
Water Supply of Poona and Kirkee with plans and estimates,
J G Fife 1866 V/23/332 no 11
The water supply of Bombay, Hector Tulloch 1872
V/27/841/4
Report on the Main Drainage of Bombay, R Aitken 1866
V/27/842/7
The Drainage and Sewage of Bombay being a Report
Submitted to the Bench of Justices of that City, H Tulloch
1872 V/27/842/8
Review of Public Works Executed by District and Local Boards,
Municipalities and other local bodies in Bengal 1894/
95 1898/99 V/24/3338

(ix) Madras and Madras Presidency
Explanation of the Municipal Commissioner regarding the
investment of sums ordered to be set apart for the draining
of the Town of Calcutta 1859 L/PJ/3/1064 no 37
Correspondence regarding the provision of public necessaries
in the vicinity of towns and stations, and the proposed enact-
ment of a law on the subject 1859 L/PWD/3/318 no 31
Correspondence regarding water supply at Calcutta; funding
and the manner in which water supply should be carried
out 1865 L/PJ/3/1095 no 47

Bibliography

PRIMARY SOURCES

(a) British Library, London
   Correspondence between Viceroys and Secretaries of State
      Florence Nightingale correspondence
(b) Bodleian Library, Oxford
   Correspondence between Viceroys and Secretaries of State
   Personal correspondence with Florence Nightingale
   Signed copy of *How People may live and not die in India*
      (Appendix 2)
(c) Cambridge University Library
   Papers of Lord Mayo including correspondence with
      Florence Nightingale
(d Florence Nightingale Museum Library, London
   Nightingale collection of letters, publications and photo-
      graphs including: 1863 Report of the Royal Commission
      on the Sanitary State of the Army in India, *with Miss
      Nightingale's observations* (Appendix 1)
   1863 (reprinted 1864) *How People may live and not die in India*

1874 *Life or Death in India*
Paper read at the National Association for the Promotion
of Social Science
1883 *The Dumb shall speak and the Deaf shall hear: or the Ryot,
the Zemindar and the Government*

SECONDARY SOURCES

Balfour, E, *The History of Lord Lytton's Indian Administration
1876-80* (Longmans Green & Co, London: 1890)
Bence-Jones, Mark, *The Viceroys of India* (Constable, London:
1982)
Benson, A C, Buckle, G E & Viscount Esher, (Editors) *The
Letters of Queen Victoria in Nine Volumes, Second Series* (John
Murray, London: 1907)
Bosworth Smith, R, *Life of Lord Lawrence, Sixth edition in Two
Volumes* (Smith, Elder & Co, London: 1885)
Buckle, G E, *The Letters of Queen Victoria, Second Series, A Selec-
tion from Her Majesty's Correspondence & Journal 1862-78, Vol I,
1862-69* (John Murray, London: 1926)
Cannadine, David, *Ornamentalism. How the British Saw Their
Empire* (Allen Lane, The Penguin Press, London: 2001)
Checkland, Sydney, *The Elgins 1766-1917: A Tale of Aristocrats,
Proconsuls & Their Wives* (Aberdeen University Press,
Aberdeen: 1988)
Cook, Edward, *The Life of Florence Nightingale, Volumes 1 & 2*
(Macmillan, London: 1913)
Cunningham, H S, *Earl Canning* (Clarendon Press: 1891)
Denholm, Anthony, *Lord Ripon 1827-1909: A Political Biography*
(Croom Helm, London: 1982)
Eden, Emily, *Up the Country* (Virago Press, London: 1983)
Ensor, Robert, *England 1870-1914* (Clarendon Press, Oxford:
1936)
Goldie, Sue M (Editor), *'I Have Done My Duty', Florence Nightingale*

in the Crimean War 1854-56 (Manchester University Press, Manchester: 1987)

Gopal, S, *The Viceroyalty of Lord Ripon, 1880-84* (Oxford University Press, London: 1953)

Gourlay, Jhanna, *Florence Nightingale & the Health of the Raj* (Ashgate, Aldershot: 2003)

Hunter, W W, T*he Life of the Earl of Mayo* (Smith, Elder & Co, London: 1875)

James, Lawrence, *The Making & Unmaking of British India* (Little, Brown & Co, London: 1997, Abacus imprint 1998)

Kaye, J W, *A History of the Sepoy War in India 1857-58, Three Volumes* (W H Allen, London: 1864-76)

Kulka, Hermann & Rothermund, Dietmar, *A History of India, Third Edition* (Routledge, London: 1998)

Lutyens, M, *The Lyttons in India* (John Murray, London: 1979)

Lyall, Alfred, *Life of the Marquis of Dufferin & Ava, Volume I* (John Murray, London: 1905)

Mallet, Bernard, *Thomas George, Earl of Northbrook* (Longmans & Co, London: 1908)

Matthew, H C G, & Harrison, Brian (Editors), *The Oxford Dictionary of National Biography in Association with the British Academy: from the earliest times to the year 2000* (Oxford University Press, Oxford: 2004)

Metcalf, Thomas R, *The Aftermath of Revolt, India 1857-70* (Princeton University Press: 1965)

Morison, J L, *The Eighth Earl of Elgin: A Chapter i7n Nineteenth Century Imperial History* (Hodder & Stoughton, London: 1928)

Newton, Lord (T W Legh), *Lord Lansdowne: A Biography* (Macmillan, London: 1929)

Oliphant, Laurence, *Narrative of the Earl of Elgin's Mission to China in the Years 1857, 1858 & 1859, Two Volumes* (W Blackwood, Edinburgh: 1860)

Pottinger, George, *Mayo, Disraeli's Viceroy* (Michael Russell (Publishing) Ltd, Salisbury, England: 1990)

Ramdin, Ron, *Mary Seacole* (Haus Publishing, London: 2005)

Seacole, Mary, *Wonderful Adventures of Mrs Seacole in Many Lands* (Blackwood, London: 1857)

Singh, H L, *Problems & Policies of the British in India 1885-1898* (Asia Publishing House, London: 1963)

Singhal, D P, *A History of the Indian People* (Methuen, London: 1983)

Spear, Percival, *A History of India* (Penguin Books, London: 1978)

Strachey, Lytton, *Eminent Victorians, with an introduction by Michael Holroyd* (Penguin Books: 1986, first published Chatto & Windus, London: 1918)

The Times, *Great Victorian Lives, An Era in Obituaries* (Times Books, London: 2007)

United States Information Service, *Village – The People* (New Delhi: 1965)

Wedderburn, William, *Florence Nightingale in India* (Contemporary Review, London: April 1914)

Woodruff, Philip, *The Men Who Ruled India, The Founders* (St Martin's Press, New York: 1954)

Woodruff, Philip, *The Men Who Ruled India, The Guardians* (St Martin's Press, New York: 1954)

Woolf, Lucien, *Life of the First Marquess of Ripon, K G, Volumes I & II* (John Murray, London: 1921)

Index

Page numbers in *italics* refer to illustrations.

Picture Sources

The author and publisher wish to express their thanks to the following sources of illustrative material and/or permission to reproduce it. They will make proper acknowledgements in future editions in the event that any omissions have occurred.